THE IMPACT OF EMERGING TECHNOLOGIES ON REFERENCE SERVICE AND BIBLIOGRAPHIC INSTRUCTION

The Impact of Emerging Technologies on Reference Service and Bibliographic Instruction

Edited by
GARY M. PITKIN

Contributions in Librarianship and Information Science, Number 87
Gerard B. McCabe, Series Adviser

GREENWOOD PRESS
Westport, Connecticut • London

Library of Congress Cataloging-in-Publication Data

The impact of emerging technologies on reference service and
   bibliographic instruction / edited by Gary M. Pitkin.
       p. cm.—(Contributions in librarianship and information
science, ISSN 0084–9243 ; no. 87)
    Includes index.
    ISBN 0–313–29365–1 (alk. paper)
     1. Reference services (Libraries)—United States.   2. Library
orientation—United States.   3. Libraries—United States—Data
processing.   4. Library information networks—United States.
5. Libraries—United States—Special collections—Databases.
I. Pitkin, Gary M.   II. Series.
Z711.I44   1995
025.5′2′0973—dc20   95–3802

British Library Cataloguing in Publication Data is available.

Library of Congress Catalog Card Number: 95–3802
ISBN: 0–313–29365–1
ISSN: 0084–9243

First published in 1995

Greenwood Press, 88 Post Road West, Westport, CT 06881
An imprint of Greenwood Publishing Group, Inc.

Printed in the United States of America

The paper used in this book complies with the
Permanent Paper Standard issued by the National
Information Standards Organization (Z39.48–1984).

10 9 8 7 6 5 4 3 2 1

Copyright Acknowledgment

The editor and publisher gratefully acknowledge permission to use extracts
from Jean Paul Emard, 1976. "An Information Science Chronology in
Perspective." *Bulletin of the American Society for Information Science* 2(8):
51–56. Used with permission from the American Society for Information
Science.

Contents

Introduction

The impetus for the collection of chapters contained in this volume arose from the realization that specific, emerging technologies are profoundly affecting the role of librarians in American society. Within the profession of librarianship, those changes appear to be most dominant in the provision of traditional reference services and bibliographic instruction. As librarians, we must be aware of the technologies involved with change and the ways in which services will be impacted. As service providers, we must be aware of the potential impacts on the people we serve. As managers, we must understand the impact of the emerging technologies on the total organization. Through the acknowledgment of these issues, we can begin to prepare for the technological future.

Equally important to the success of librarianship is the ability of library schools to prepare future librarians for the reality of technological change. Library educators must fully understand the impact of the emerging technologies on traditional services and must train students accordingly. The library school curriculum must focus on change and emphasize the ability of graduates to manage information in non-traditional environments incorporating non-traditional methodologies. This will require a restructuring of traditional programs and the employment of non-traditional methods of teaching that will expose students to the changing technological environment. Also, because information is now an international commodity, educators must emphasize the international development of librarianship.

To this end, the chapters are organized into two distinct units. The first addresses "The Technological Effect on Library Service." George Machovec sets the tone in the initial chapter for eventual identification of technological impacts on reference service and bibliographic instruction. He does so by identifying the most significant of the emerging technologies. Discussed in detail are the role and function of consortia, locally loaded databases, community files, graphics, imaging and multimedia, networking, client-server architecture, graphical user interfaces, and advanced document delivery techniques.

Johannah Sherrer and Harvey Sager follow Machovec's introduction to the specific emerging technologies with analyses of the implications on reference service and bibliographic instruction. Sherrer addresses technological impacts on the traditional reference services by stating that "New technologies are requiring that reference departments reevaluate hours of operation, staffing levels, the degree of specialization, relationships with other types of libraries, other internal library departments, and the assumptions underlying institutional uniqueness." She also provides strategies for incorporating new and emerging technologies into reference services and strategies for assessing the implications of technological applications. Within this context, she calls for "reference services to move beyond bibliographic access toward actual document delivery by accepting responsibility for providing both documents and information. This should mean actually securing documents, through locating the exact information requested and retrieving it simultaneously."

Harvey Sager follows Johannah Sherrer with a similar analysis of the impact of emerging technologies on bibliographic instruction. He describes the pressures of technological change as "the best case for course-integrated library instruction and the creation of an environment where librarians have contact with classes over time, and information skills are learned incrementally." Through an analysis of what we teach, how we teach, and why we teach, Sager concludes that "Whether one believes that information literacy is an educational revolution, a mid-course correction, or the latest reworked educational slogan, the march of technology will demand that we articulate a new reason to teach that builds upon and then moves beyond our current short-term, short-retention, technology skill-based teaching objectives."

The impact of emerging technologies on reference services and bibliographic instruction is discussed in terms of library clientele and library personnel by John Tyson and Delmus Williams. Tyson emphasizes the library's role and responsibility in creating an information literate society. The sophistication of the emerging technologies will allow that role to develop incrementally over time and substantially influence curriculum reform and customer service. "Every library in America will have a role to play in ensuring that library clientele who need or wish to improve their information literacy skills have the opportunity to do so. . . . Libraries must continue to play a proactive role in assuring equitable access and use of information systems regardless of the library client's social and economic status."

According to Delmus Williams, library managers are ultimately responsible for the successful integration of the emerging technologies into the daily operation of traditional services. "The capacity of information technology to tailor information to the needs of the user is making the way librarians and others have approached information management obsolete." Not only does technology impact the provision of services, it changes the way library's are budgeted, staffed, and marketed. Managers must approach personnel with commitments to staff development, job security, and self-esteem.

Charles Lowry wraps up the first unit of this volume by providing a provocative synopsis on "Preparing for the Technological Future." He focuses his analysis on the information technology infrastructure, the virtual library tool kit, and prototypes and problems at Carnegie Mellon University. The emphasis is on building "a foundation of information technologies that allows users to access electronic information easily." This philosophy is addressed through the statement that "we must understand the psychology of human information-seeking behaviors, and we must shape the systems through this understanding."

The second unit, "The Technological Effect on Library Education," is designed to build on the importance of the emerging technologies in relationship to the preparation of future librarians to ensure success in the changing environment. As the emerging technologies will impact heavily on the provision of reference services and bibliographic instruction, they will equally impact the library school curriculum, methods of teaching, the librarian of the future as information professional, and the international development of librarianship.

In the initial chapter of this unit, Thomas Walker states that "Technological obsolescence threatens library and information science just as it does other professions and disciplines with important technological components. To convey a sense of the evolving nature of technologies is one of the many objectives of library education." In terms of curricular growth and the methodologies of teaching, Walker contends that "the evolving nature of technologies" is conveyed through library education understanding and teaching conceptions of technology, the changing functions of technology, and professional competencies. He identifies courses that should emphasize technology and defines "the place of library education and research in a period of rapid technological innovation." Within the scope of the second concept, he presents models of knowledge and defines the symbiosis between libraries and library education.

Herbert Achleitner complements Walker's emphasis on curricular change with an emphasis on the need to train and prepare "information professionals" for the emerging technological environment. The role, indeed the definition, of the traditional librarian is changing. Achleitner addresses this concept through descriptions of the information society, impetus for change, emerging paradigms, information technologies and organizations, information professionals, knowledge management, and educational trends.

Charles Conaway concludes this volume with a detailed discussion of the impacts of emerging technologies on the international development of librarianship. Library education in the United States plays a major role in this arena as the vast majority of library professionals on an international scale receive their degrees in this country. After the presentation of factors influencing the diffusion of technological innovation in libraries on an international level, Conaway discusses the implications of library education on the development of international librarianship. This is followed by a description of activities of specific organizations involved with the international development of librarianship. Problems and strategies involved with preparing students to return to their own countries following graduation from U.S. library schools are also presented.

The intent of this volume is to assist in the understanding of emerging technologies and the role they will play in the provision of reference services and bibliographic instruction. Ancillary to this intent is the necessity of library education to be a partner with libraries to ensure the future success of librarianship in serving the public.

THE IMPACT OF EMERGING TECHNOLOGIES ON REFERENCE SERVICE AND BIBLIOGRAPHIC INSTRUCTION

1 Identifying Emerging Technologies

George Machovec

The virtual library is no longer merely the dream of a few visionaries or information scientists but is emerging in many ways, shapes, and forms. However, many of the building blocks of this dream are not yet assembled into a finished product—and many libraries merely have a pile of unrelated building blocks (i.e., products and services) not presented to the user in a fully coherent fashion. Libraries around the world are moving into a host of projects and services that support the electronic access to information both inside and outside library walls. These changes are having a profound effect on how librarians view themselves and how they offer services. This chapter will focus on some of the significant emerging technologies that are affecting the very heart of reference service and bibliographic instruction. The purpose is not to present a comprehensive analysis in all areas of library automation and networking, which is impossible in this format, but to provide some broad brushstrokes on some of the major trends in the field.

CONSORTIUM

Library consortia are playing an increasingly important role in the implementation of emerging technologies in libraries. There are many reasons for this phenomena, including the leveraging of funds for database licensing, the enlarged access to information for the patron, a greater voice with integrated library system vendors, the advantages of volume purchases, the sharing of expertise and training, the ability to do special projects that no one member could afford, the increased possibilities for outside funding, and better services for patrons and the use of shared personnel for system and network management. Although this appears to contradict current movement toward distributed computing, it is actually complementary.

The role of consortia in automated resource sharing can be an important element for extending and using technology. However, it is not a panacea in every instance and participants must go into partnerships in an intelligent manner. According to Bernard G. Sloan (1991: vii):

> Automated resource sharing is not an absolute good. Many supporters portray it as a moral imperative, as something that should be accepted on faith. That is a dangerous position. Libraries should enter into automated resource sharing with both eyes open. Library managers should weigh the pros and cons and decide how to proceed based on a careful evaluation of alternatives, always keeping the patron in mind. Done correctly, automated resource sharing can greatly benefit patrons by providing access to library materials that are not held locally. Done incorrectly, attempts at automated resource sharing can end in disaster. A program can be underutilized and overpriced, draining precious dollars from tight library budgets with no appreciable benefits.

Database Licensing

It is a common practice among database producers to provide discounts to consortia or other groups of libraries for multiple licensing of database subscriptions. Sometimes these discounts are available only if the product is centrally mounted and provided to several sites through a shared server. In any event, groups of libraries hold much greater sway over database producers for special pricing arrangements than if an institution independently negotiates a contract.

Broadened Patron Access

Increased patron access to a body of library catalogs, databases, and other products and services is probably the most compelling reason for libraries to cooperate. Offering this access through a single shared automated system or through a series of local linked systems, via the Internet or other networking techniques, is one of the primary reasons for cooperation. Advanced document delivery opportunities, shared borrowing privileges, and ubiquitous access to electronic resources are key benefits.

Influence with Integrated Library System Vendors

Most vendors of integrated library systems (ILS) are strongly influenced by their client base for the future direction of system development and bug resolution. It is not uncommon for vendors to perform annual surveys, get input from user groups, and conduct development under implementation and performance contracts. Library consortia can play an especially influential role with vendors because they represent a body of clients that wield financial and political muscle. Properly harnessed, this power can be used to cause system changes and open the doors for partnering opportunities that may not be possible from a single institution. This group leveraging with vendors is even more important for small- to medium-sized libraries, which will have little influence if they act independently.

Volume Purchasing

Most libraries, except the very largest, have the dilemma that they are not able to take advantage of bulk or volume purchasing of computer hardware, peripherals, library supplies, or printed materials. The ability to leverage purchasing power through a central cooperative can be very attractive. For example, the acquisition of large quantities of microcomputers at the same time can bring significant savings to each individual member.

Training and Continuing Education

Through pooling institutional expertise and hiring centralized staff and consultants, many consortia are able to provide training, continuing education, and consulting services far beyond what a single site can afford. These types of continuing education programs are beneficial to both staff and patrons.

Special Projects

Many customized automation projects come with high price tags and the need for specialized talent. In addition, vendors are more likely to want to develop partnering opportunities with groups of libraries to take advantage of economies-of-scale and avoid the development of "parochial" solutions, which benefit only a single site. Once again, through the pooling of funds, the bringing together of expertise, and the power of collective requirements, special joint projects are more likely in a consortial environment.

Shared System and Network Management

Personnel expenses traditionally absorb the largest percentage of any library's budget. Through the implementation of a shared automated system, many libraries are able to lower personnel costs through the sharing of a common hardware and software platform along with the shared expenses for staff to manage the system and the network.

LOCALLY LOADED DATABASES

Libraries have a growing number of technological options for providing access to databases and information services. The issue is more than the simple selection of databases and involves a solution for "how" access will be provided. Different solutions have balancing sets of pros and cons, which must be examined for ease of use, user interfaces, power of the search engine, cost, number of concurrent users, telecommunications flexibility, database availability, and licensing costs.

Typical choices include the mounting of databases on a local online public access catalog (OPAC), gatewaying to commercial vendors (e.g., EPIC, FirstSearch, RLG's Citadel, CARL Systems Inc., DRANET, Dialog Information Services), establishing independent servers (e.g., UNIX based) connected to the institutional network or OPAC and the networking of CD-ROMs (compact disk–random-access memories). In many cases, libraries may select several choices depending on their priorities and budget.

Loading Databases on the Local OPAC

The loading of databases in the local OPAC has been one of the hottest trends in the last decade. With the ability of local vendors to support this type of activity through software coupled with lower costs for computer hardware and disk space, even small- and medium-sized institutions have moved in this direction. The trend became so predominant by the late 1980s (Potter 1989: 99–104; Machovec 1989: 161–171) that an entire issue of *Information Technology and Libraries* (June 1989) was devoted to the subject. The local loading of indexing/abstracting services, reference tools, statistical files, and other products is not subsiding but has become standard for many automated library systems.

Advantages

- Local control over what to load, how to load it, and frequency of updates (within choices supported by the database producer)
- The same search engine and interface as the library catalogs
- Multiple users from many workstations can simultaneously use the files
- Takes advantage of the existing communications network and terminal pool
- The files can be available over the Internet or through dial-up with appropriate networking and security
- Databases of local or regional interest can be created or loaded as needed, although the necessary disk, setup, and loading expenses may need to be paid

Disadvantages

- Institution must pay directly for necessary disk
- There may be a cost for the database loader
- The OPAC search engine may be inadequate for some databases
- If sites outside the library or consortia want access to the file, the owner will need to determine policies and fees for vending the product within licensing restrictions by the database producer

Networked CD-ROMs

The networking of CD-ROMs within a library system or campus represents one of the most popular trends in library automation today. Not only are many popular indexing and abstracting tools available in this format, but the explosion of multimedia books on CD-ROM is just taking off. The CD-ROM format is here to stay, but it should be used where appropriate with other automation technologies.

Advantages

- Limited number of simultaneous user access (generally ten or less concurrent users)
- Can easily be networked in a building local area network (LAN)
- Can have customized search engine to best suit the file
- Moderately low cost for intermediate number of users

Disadvantages

- Number of simultaneous users is limited by slower CD-ROM access speeds
- Although network access is easy in a LAN environment, it is much more difficult to offer wide area network (WAN) access because of the proprietary nature of LAN technology and the need for special client software packages
- Different search engines and interfaces for different product lines
- LAN management can be time consuming for local staff

Distributed UNIX Servers

Distributed servers using the UNIX operating system are becoming a popular methodology for providing database and network access. A number of vendors now provide not only the search software but also preindexed databases for easy loading and maintenance (e.g., Ovid by CD-Plus, BRS/Search, InfoShare by NOTIS). In addition, libraries are increasingly making use, on the same servers, of a variety of network management and access tools such as Gopher, Veronica, and World-Wide Web. The relatively low cost of UNIX hardware and disk space make this technology a popular option for many automation projects. Also, the UNIX operating system is well understood and many of the applications, programming languages, and programming tools are widely taught.

Advantages

- Relatively low cost hardware including central processing unit (CPU) and disk space
- Employs a distributed computing technology putting servers where needed most
- Easy to network over the Internet
- Z39.50 support for some search packages
- Graphical user interfaces often available
- Other networking technology is available, which may broaden the applications for the UNIX server (e.g., Gopher)

Disadvantages

- The licensing of a search engine can be very expensive and may need to be done over and over again, depending on how many servers and concurrent users are needed
- Local site management of the machine will take time and expertise
- Loaders may need to be developed if not available "off the shelf"

Gateways to Databases and Systems over the Network

Another popular trend is not to locally load databases at all but to provide gateway access to databases loaded on another system on the network or commercial service. Not only are traditional database utilities participating in this market (e.g., Dialog Information Services, STN International, BRS) but also vendors such as OCLC (FirstSearch and EPIC), RLIN (Citadel), WLN, CARL Corporation, and others.

One of the most interesting new types of services to become available on the network in the last few years has been the "table of contents" indexing services as pioneered by the CARL Corporation (their UnCover services, which is a joint project with B.H. Blackwell, indexes over 17,000 titles and has over 6 million records as of mid-1994). UnCover has been such a success that it has been cloned by several other companies such as OCLC's ContentsFirst, Faxon's ArticleExpress, and the British Lending Library's Inside Information (offered through vendors such as EBSCO and RLG). Most of the products are primarily used over the Internet on a gateway basis.

Advantages

- No large up-front costs for search engine or hardware
- Another vendor is responsible for maintaining the system and updating the databases
- A wide array of files may be available, particularly if more than one vendor is being used

Disadvantages

- There may be relatively high costs for searching whether it be per search (e.g., FirstSearch or EPIC), per concurrent user licensing, or by connect time or hit charges. This discourages high-volume use and facilitates difficult decisions on financing and cost recovery.
- Depending on the type of network access employed, there may be some limitations on the number of concurrent users.
- If more than one system is being used, the user will have multiple search interfaces and engines.
- Z39.50 compliance is available on some but not all systems.

Print

To be complete, one must always include the traditional printed format for access to information!

Advantages

- No hardware and software costs
- Easy to use
- Can be read almost anywhere
- High-quality resolution for graphics and print

Disadvantages

- No distributed network access is possible without digitizing (at high cost and with possible copyright restrictions).
- Printed indexes can be very slow to use, especially when coordinating several concepts.
- Reduced number of access points as compared with online tools.
- Updates to some printed indexes and directories are less frequent than online counterparts.
- If a product is a reference tool then it must be used in the library.

COMMUNITY FILES

For many years libraries have maintained local information and referral files to assist with reference services. These have begun to migrate from cards to personal computers (PCs)—and now many libraries are putting these types of files on OPACs to provide open, public use. Libraries must grapple with a number of key issues in creating community files such as who creates and maintains the file, restrictions on use, how the data are entered (or uploaded), and associated costs. Many interesting types of projects and databases have been developed in local library systems in meeting community information needs.

Who Creates and Maintains the File

Everyone is receptive to the idea of creating databases of local or regional interest. It is easy to establish a list of wonderful ideas. It is not so easy to handle issues associated with developing and maintaining the file. Quite often, the people who create the ideas are not the individuals responsible for bringing the concept to fruition. Also, not all OPAC vendors support the creation of local community files. Although data may be available electronically from a publisher; company; research institute; local, state, or federal government agency; or other source, the development of a loader program can become extremely complex. The complexities involved should be seriously examined before any agreement is reached to establish a local file.

Another trend in this arena is the emergence of community Free-Nets, many of which are modeled after the original "Cleveland Free-net" developed by Tom Grundner. (Bryn 1993: 19+; Balas 1993: 28+; Machovec 1990: 1–4). In addition, Campus-Wide Information Systems (CWIS) are the rage in most academic institutions. In some cases, these are managed by the library, but more often they are established by the computer center. Typically, these are created through Gopher software, which can be easily mounted on UNIX servers on campus.

Interesting Ideas with Community Files

Many interesting and creative local databases have been developed. These include some of the following types:

- Child care and elder care directories
- State legislative databases of all new bills, status of bills, and legislative newsletters
- Local authors
- Local/regional economic statistics
- Calendar of events
- Local agencies and clubs
- Local and state documents
- Arts database
- City council agenda and minutes
- Press releases of the campus or community
- Career service and job opportunities
- Map index
- Index of popular songs
- Local newspaper index

GRAPHICS, IMAGING, AND MULTIMEDIA

We live in a multimedia society where the average citizen has come to expect the full range of text, graphics, sound, still images, animation, and videos. At the same time, libraries have expanded collection development priorities to include in addition to traditional print, videos, CDs, CD-ROMs, videodisks, software, and other formats. Libraries have also begun

to acquire multimedia, optical disk products such as encyclopedias, interactive videodisks and other products. Many vendors of integrated online
library systems (IOLS) are actively incorporating graphics, imaging, and
multimedia capabilities into local systems.

The Multimedia Advantage

Anyone who has had the opportunity to use a well-designed multimedia
product quickly becomes addicted. Many types of information can be
presented quite effectively with products that engage multiple senses in
the information seeker. Multimedia technology is being heavily main-
streamed in the secondary education system and is making major impacts
in higher education as well. Multimedia systems are being used not only
for presentations but also for individualized instruction. Multimedia offers
the user the ability to control learning to an unprecedented degree; users
can employ different media to match learning styles.

Trends in Multimedia for the IOLS

As repositories of information, libraries have a special role in information literacy, research, preserving information, recreation, and education.
The integrated library system is the center tool for managing the activities
of a library. A number of interesting trends and issues are emerging relating
to multimedia use in the IOLS:

- Since multimedia technology requires huge telecommunications bandwidths
  for distribution, a significant investment will be required for data communications to use these technologies in areas wider than a LAN.
- Traditionally, "dumb terminals" have been used as workstations for text-based
  OPACs. Libraries that are planning for the future will begin to migrate to DOS,
  Macintosh, or UNIX workstations for end-user access to the OPAC.
- It is becoming much cheaper to distribute computing on smaller platforms. A
  central mainframe is not needed to house everything. Appropriate products
  must be placed on a platform that is sized to meet expected applications, which
  are then networked to provide in-house and remote access. The key is
  networking!
- National standards must be followed whenever possible in the building of a
  multimedia system. This is especially important if an organization wants to
  open external access to its multimedia products over the Internet or other
  networks.

- The first step for many vendors is the linking of images to records in an OPAC database. The CARL Corporation, VTLS, Innovative Interfaces, and others have limited products already on the market in this area. For example, the CARL Corporation will allow the library to link scanned TIFF (tagged image file format) images to bibliographic records, which may be stored on a local LAN or on the OPAC minicomputer. One advantage of storing such images on a local LAN rather than a minicomputer or a mainframe computer is that disk storage is much cheaper on LANs than on traditional mainframes.
- Because it is expensive to produce multimedia products and store scanned images, libraries will need to cooperate and network on projects and not duplicate efforts.
- Intellectual property rights and copyright in the networked, multimedia environment can be especially difficult. Great care and attention will need to be paid to this issue before mounting a product or beginning a project.
- Censorship issues can also be sensitive in the multimedia environment. Libraries have always had difficulties with censorship, even in the print environment. This can be amplified with graphics, video, and audio.

Conclusion

Funding for automation projects is limited in these difficult economic times. Libraries need to balance provisions for greater access to text-based information systems as opposed to limited-scale, multimedia products or projects. However, as libraries move into the twenty-first century, full-range, multimedia integrated library systems will become a necessity rather than a luxury.

NETWORKING

The linking and networking of library and information systems represents one of the greatest priorities of library automation today. In the same way that no library can physically own all materials in some topic or format, no library can locally load or maintain all databases. The networking of library and information systems provides the opportunity for libraries to greatly enhance access to information in local, regional, national, and international systems.

Some of the interesting trends shaping this area are databases and systems on the Internet (Gophers, wide area information servers [WAIS], World-Wide Web [WWW]), private networks developed by vendors (e.g., CARL Systems and DRAnet), consortia networking through the sharing of a common system, local networking, linking CD-ROMs and other optical products to library OPACs, and the evolution of LANs and WANs.

The Internet

The Internet refers to more than 5,000 backbone, regional and local computer networks in more than 100 countries with an estimated user base of over several million people. The term "Information Highway," referring to the National Research and Education Network (NREN), which is being supported by the Clinton Administration, is becoming a common term in many popular publications. It provides the promise of a high-speed, electronic highway for all Americans. Control and funding are major political issues that have not been settled.

The network is growing at such a phenomenal pace that its extent and diversity are not understood. A host of directories, information servers, products, and navigational tools are presently available and many more are in development. To the newcomer on the "Net," even the names of some of the different gateways, products, and services sound unusual and can be very confusing. These include Gophers, Archie, Veronica, HYTELNET, WAIS, WWW, and Mosaic.

The Electronic Journal

The network has spawned an entirely new information distribution industry. The emergence of electronic journals, which are not formally published in printed form, are presenting new challenges to libraries. The dichotomy of information "haves" and "have nots" becomes critical, since these electronic journals are accessible only to those on the network. In addition, libraries and database producers need to develop methods for archiving and indexing these electronic publications so that they are accessible to future generations.

Gopher

The Gopher is a distributed networking and document delivery system designed to work across any Transmission Control Protocol/International Protocol (TCP/IP) network. It was originally developed in 1991 by the University of Minnesota Microcomputer, Workstation, and Networks Center to assist campus users in accessing electronic information and navigating the Internet. The product, well designed and simple to use, was soon recognized as the Campus-Wide Information System (CWIS) at the

University of Minnesota. It has since been distributed and cloned at many Internet sites around the world.

The Gopher system has two major pieces: the server software and the client software. The server accepts queries from users and responds by going to a menu, delivering a document, offering gateway access over the Internet, saving a file, and/or printing it. Gopher, specifically designed to move away from expensive mainframe technology, supports server software designed to work in the UNIX environment on a number of different platforms. These server packages are public domain, hence their popularity. A Gopher server may be accessed from a VT100 compatible terminal emulation device or from a number of graphical user interface (GUI) clients, which are available under Macintosh, Windows, and X Windows operating systems.

Archie

Three of the major types of data traffic on the Internet include interactive terminal sessions (telnet), file transfers (using the file transfer protocol [FTP]) and electronic mail. Thousands of organizations have provided software, data files, images, textual information, and other data on the Internet for access by anyone on the network. Identifying availability became a significant problem especially with the rapid expansion of the network.

Archie, the McGill School of Computer Science Archive Server Listing Service, is a tool developed to help solve the identification problem. Archie actually consists of two software tools: the first keeps track of Internet FTP archive sites in a central server and is updated about once per month; the second allows users to query this database to identify who owns what. Users may access an Archie server (many are now available on the network) to find where different files are available for downloading.

Veronica

Veronica is a UNIX-based service that provides an index of titles of items on gopher servers around the world. To use Veronica, a user must be logged-on to a gopher client from which a search request is initiated. The result of the search is a set of Gopher-type data items, which are returned to the user in the form of a Gopher menu. The user can then access any of the data by selecting from the returned menu.

Veronica offers a keyword search of most Gopher-server menus in the entire Gopher web. As Archie is to FTP archives, Veronica is to Gopherspace. Unlike Archie, the search results can be connected directly to the data source. Because Veronica is accessed through a Gopher client, it is easy to use and gives access to all types of data supported by the Gopher protocol.

Veronica was designed as a response to the problem of resource discovery in the rapidly expanding Gopher web. Frustrated comments in the net news groups have recently reflected the need for such a service. Additional motivation came from the comments of naive Gopher users, several of whom assumed that a simple-to-use service would provide a means to find resources "without having to know where they are."

Wide Area Information Server

The WAIS project began as an experimental venture among Thinking Machines Corporation, Apple Computer, Dow Jones & Company, and KPMG Peat Marwick. The purpose was to create an easy-to-use interface that could access many information servers on the Internet, regardless of location. WAIS uses client/server architecture based on an extension of the Z39.50 NISO (National Information Standards Organization) protocol. Two components are necessary: WAIS servers and WAIS client software. Interaction with the WAIS system occurs through the Question Interface, which is a graphical user interface piece of client software. To begin a session, the user asks a question, pulls down a menu identifying servers that will be queried (the WAIS software can also identify source systems if the user does not know what to select), and then sends the query. After the appropriate information is retrieved from the remote servers, headlines of materials are displayed in a window and the user selects the relevant information.

World-Wide Web

The WWW is one of the newest access tools. The initial design was conducted as CERN, the European Particle Physics Laboratory in Geneva, Switzerland. As with the other navigational tools, developments with the WWW are in a dynamic state of change that has expanded well beyond the initiating organization.

Basically, WWW is an effort to organize information on the Internet, plus local information, into a set of hypertext documents. Navigation through the network is conducted by moving from one document to another via a set of hypertext links.

The WWW may be used via a "line-oriented" front-end, called a "browser," or a loaded WWW client developed for NeXT UNIX workstations, X Window systems (one is called Viola and another ViolaWWW), or Macintosh or MS-DOS PCs. Copies of these client software packages are available via anonymous FTP from the address info.cern.ch in the directory pub/WWW/bin. The WWW software has been placed in the public domain by CERN so that more rapid development of this resource could occur over the network.

Mosaic

The Mosaic graphical user interface was developed by the National Center for Supercomputing Applications (NCSA) at the University of Illinois and supports easy access to documents, graphics, and other forms of multimedia over the Internet. The software capitalizes on the World-Wide Web product developed at CERN, which enables the use of hypertext links to jump to different documents on the network. The advantage of the Mosaic graphical user interface is that it uses hot links to photographs, video sequences, or other graphics and not just text. It was originally developed for the X Window environment (UNIX), but client packages are now in wide distribution for Macintosh and Windows operating systems. Because of the wide-scale interest in this interface as a network navigation tool, a number of integrated library system vendors have already incorporated Mosaic into their public access catalog (PAC) graphical user interfaces.

CLIENT-SERVER ARCHITECTURE

Computing is moving toward a distributed architecture. In this environment, the user should not need to care or know where information is stored. From a single workstation, the user should be able to move among systems finding relevant information to meet research needs. In addition, libraries need to design and plan for the future of universal connectivity for the electronic library.

A client-server system offers a number of advantages over traditional dumb-terminal-to-host configurations. First, more powerful functionality can be developed for the searcher, since software development on the client computer is generally easier to implement. This minimizes host computer development (always more difficult) and allows the larger systems to work as servers for the clients.

Second, a familiar and common user interface can be developed to interact with each of the host machines. In a microcomputer environment, it is also easier to develop graphical user interfaces, which can make end-user interfaces easier to use. Predictions exist that the command-driven Common Command Language (Z39.58) may be somewhat obsolete for end-user searching since GUIs make front-ends more practical. Third, it is easier to provide a common mechanism for downloading large amounts of data from a server and conduct local processing on the client computer, thus lowering the load on the host computer.

Fourth, much of the computing power is shifted from the centralized mainframe or minicomputer to the remote client computer. One misconception is that the client-server architecture needs less computer power. This is generally not the case, since some of the computing is now distributed to the client machine.

Fifth, application programs (i.e., search engines) may be tailored to best meet the needs for the database in question (e.g., bibliographic, full text, numeric, graphic), and the common user access and interface is developed for the client computer. This implies that the best hardware and software at the lowest cost may be employed to meet a particular organization's information needs regardless of platform.

How Should Libraries Respond?

Obviously, a great deal of work is currently in the development stage for client-server architectures. To best plan for the future of more universal connectivity, libraries should begin to move in the following directions:

- Microcomputers should be acquired rather than "dumb terminals" as workstations for library systems and other types of library connectivity. This will allow the development of client software for the end-user.
- It is best to avoid "direct connected" workstations to a host computer. Rather, connections through an organizational backbone or hardware which allows switched virtual circuits will allow switching among host computers as client-server applications become available in an institution.
- As libraries develop request for proposals (RFPs) for new information systems, it will be important to request that Z39.50 client-server architectures be offered from the vendor. Although these types of protocols cannot yet be listed as mandatory, development and interest by the vendor should be sought.

GRAPHICAL USER INTERFACES

The era of end-user command-driven systems is quickly passing. Online systems are moving from command-driven and simple menu systems toward graphical user interfaces, which provide a common front-end for a variety of information systems. The trends in this arena have been set by microcomputer products such as Windows, Macintosh, HyperCard, and other tools that have shaped our understanding of effective user interfaces.

Virtually every major developer of integrated library systems is developing such interfaces. As this segment of the industry matures, there will be a growing array of specialty products. For example, the CARL Corporation has developed "The Kid's Catalog," which provides an interface to the CARL software for children. This trend will continue as specialty pieces of client software are developed for kids, adults, ADA (Americans with Disabilities Act) compliance, and for specialized databases.

As national standards such as the Z39.50 protocol are incorporated into host servers, the possibility for the user to select Z39.50 software from a variety of vendors will increase. This will allow users to select the interface they most prefer. One difficulty is that the search capabilities on many OPACs exceed what the basic Z39.50 protocol supports, and there is not always a one-to-one correlation between a search on one system to another. This means that the client software developed for a particular host may work best on its "native" system.

ADVANCED DOCUMENT DELIVERY TECHNIQUES

The long-term goal in providing document delivery is the real-time electronic delivery of a document directly to the patron in the library, home, or office. This service is available with selected products from a limited number of vendors. Ubiquitous access to this type of information delivery, however, is far from reality because of copyright restrictions, the lack of machine-readable copy for large numbers of older materials, the lack of an advanced telecommunications infrastructure, and the costs of providing local delivery mechanisms and workstations.

As a related element, many of the traditional delivery systems (e.g., interlibrary loan) are being upgraded to provide better and faster access to materials. This may include the ability for patrons to order materials at a network (or OPAC) terminal and have the items delivered in a relatively short timeframe to their nearest library, home or office.

Traditionally, "interlibrary loan" (ILL) services refer to library-to-library interaction for borrowing and lending materials and the provision of photocopies of journal articles or shorter monographic works. Although libraries still maintain ILL departments, the move toward rapid patron-initiated document delivery services are changing the landscape of traditional services. A number of important trends are radically changing the ILL and document delivery arena. This is causing many libraries and consortia to recast their vision of what document delivery services should entail in the next decade.

Important Trends Affecting Traditional ILL and Document Delivery

During the last few years, a number of major shifts have been occurring in the information and library automation marketplace along with many technological advances, which are combining to significantly alter how libraries are planning their futures.

- Rapidly rising prices of many serial titles are forcing libraries to cancel subscriptions and rely on alternative mechanisms for article delivery. Access rather than ownership is becoming increasingly important.
- The increase of table-of-contents (TOC) indexing services, which offer content listings with almost no lag time after an issue's release and reasonably priced full-text delivery of indexed articles, is a compelling alternative for libraries and patrons alike. UnCover, which began in 1988 as the first such service, now indexes over 17,000 journal titles and provides most articles in 24 hours or less via fax. UnCover also provides a growing number of articles in under 1 hour through the employment of advanced scanning and storage techniques. Based on this success, other companies have cloned this service into OCLC's ContentsFirst, Faxon's ArticleExpress, and the British Library's TOC service.
- Fax technology has become ubiquitous in most libraries and in many homes and offices.
- The delivery of images and text over the Internet has become commonplace with projects such as RLG's Ariel service.
- The ILL subsystems of Online Computer Library Center (OCLC), Research Library Information Network (RLIN), and other major utilities have become the basis for phenomenal numbers of transactions. By early 1994, OCLC has supported almost 50 million transactions through their ILL subsystem alone.
- Many vendors are beginning to offer significant numbers of scanned article images on CD-ROM for local library use or connecting through local or regional networks. For example, UMI's ProQuest for Business scans some 500

business and economic journals and puts the CD-ROM disks in a jukebox for easy delivery and printing after identifying articles through the ABI/INFORM database. Organizations are now beginning to offer this fast delivery service in a networked environment.

- Many libraries and library consortia are using integrated library systems that build patron-initiated document delivery services into PAC interfaces. Patrons are increasingly able to order materials directly from publishers and from table-of-contents indexing services similar to UnCover. They can also request that books be delivered to the local library without visiting an ILL desk or initiating any forms.

A November 1992 report entitled *Maximizing Access, Minimizing Cost: A First Step Toward the Information Access Future* identified a vision of the "ideal" system:

The "ideal" is a system which furthers patron self-sufficiency by supporting patron-initiated document requests, with the products (books, articles, videos . . .) going quickly, directly, and reliably to the patron. Requests are routed to the most cost effective alternative, whether it is a library, a document supplier such as CARL or UMI, or another as-yet-unknown and perhaps electronic source. Cost effective alternatives are assured by a competitive environment.

Fees for a university's community would be absorbed by the "library" or its replacement and be part of the university's information budget, which includes provisions for purchasing traditional materials, licensing data and electronic publications, and borrowing or purchasing information for patrons. Non-profit net "lenders" could be compensated in some way by net "borrowers."

In the ideal system, resource sharing is a central rather than a marginal service. Patrons are encouraged to use resource sharing services, through placement and advertisement of the services and through guaranteed timely filling of their needs. Resource sharing staff are more productive because significant parts of the resource sharing efforts are taken on by patrons and by library-designed technological links and filters. Local online catalogs will, if a patron searches for an item lacking locally, provide the option of a search of other sources of supply (national bibliographic utilities or commercial suppliers), with the forwarding of a request to obtain the item either to the library's resource sharing staff or directly to the supplier, with billing and management information captured for local system handling.

Resource sharing is a cost to the library rather than the patron and equal to reference, acquisitions, cataloging—services historically provided at no cost to the patron. No library feels exploited by others. Ranking of Association of Research (ARL) Libraries reflects the effects of resource sharing on service to local patrons and on support of scholarship worldwide. Authors and publishers are fairly paid for their works. (Baker and Jackson 1992: 17pp)

In another example of an effort in this area, the Colorado Alliance of Research Libraries adopted a goal statement for the development of an advanced patron-initiated document delivery system in a virtual library setting that will provide the user with the perception of accessing "one library." Although the project is just in the conceptual stage and will be built over several years, it closely parallels, in concept, the ARL "ideal system" but would be built regionally. Some of the characteristics of the document delivery system include

- Alliance patrons will be able to initiate from any PAC terminal, Internet session, or dial-in session the ability to request a book or article from any library in the Alliance. The item, for a fee, would then be delivered to the nearest local participating library or the patron's home or office.
- Patrons will be able to request, at cost, any document type (e.g., journal article, conference paper, standard). Ideally, the user should be able to order a document from any database that covers bibliographic citations and be presented with appropriate delivery options with corresponding delivery mechanisms along with costs and delivery times.
- The software will perform all routing for document delivery requests based on acceptable protocols to Alliance libraries.
- The software will interface with other document delivery systems when requests need to go outside the Alliance. This ability to interface with other document suppliers or library systems is predicated on the use of national protocols and standards.
- Appropriate report and management statistics will be available to Alliance libraries from the software.
- The Alliance will develop clear and equitable borrowing privileges to the extent that patrons are "virtually" accessing "one library" when using any Alliance library catalog.
- The long-term goal will be to provide as many documents as possible in an online, real-time mode at workstations in the library or via high-speed dial-in or network links. This will mitigate the human effort in existing ILL departments. This may occur at increasing levels through the use of scanned articles

in UnCover as well as implementing other scanned document services which will be interfaced through PAC (e.g., UMI's ProQuest, products from IAC, Project Adonis, scanned images directly from publishers, among others).

North American Interlibrary Loan/Document Delivery Project

The emphasis being placed on document delivery (DD) initiatives has been so pervasive in the library community that the Association of Research Libraries, the Council on Library Resources (CLR), and the University of Pennsylvania, among others, have begun a new collaborative project called the North American Interlibrary Loan/Document Delivery Project (NAILDD). The goal of the project is to disassemble and reconstruct ILL and document delivery services in an electronic environment. Some of the specific objectives of the project are to encourage internal management of ILL/DD services, streamline billing services in the electronic environment, and provide electronic linkages between local and national systems.

The initiative began in 1991 as a result of the activities of the ARL Committee on Access to Information Resources. Two white papers were produced—the October 1991 "Evolution of Electronic Resource Sharing" and the November 1992 "Maximizing Access, Minimizing Costs: A First Step Toward the Information Access Future." On September 10, 1993, the NAILDD convened a meeting between interested libraries and automation vendors and developed the "North American Interlibrary Loan/Document Delivery Project: ILL/DD Management System Description," which describes a list of the major features and technical requirements to be incorporated into any state-of-the-art ILL and DD system in the electronic environment.

Conclusion

The building of modern document delivery systems that empower the patron to identify and request materials in a convenient, timely, and cost effective manner is the key to the information future of libraries. The producers of integrated library systems and the national utilities need to work together to ensure compatibility in a multivendor environment. Patrons need to be offered flexibility and choice in selecting how materials will be delivered in terms of mechanisms, price, and time. To fully accomplish these goals, systems must be built around national standards for ILL, telecommunications, serial identification, patron record information, and circulation transactions.

STANDARDS

Standards represent one of the hallmarks of progress and maturity of any technology. The Machine Readable Cataloging (MARC) record has become the basis for virtually all library information systems. However, as libraries move into the twenty-first century, a host of other standards in computing, telecommunications, information retrieval, and other areas affect our system design. Some of the major standards that do or will affect library automation include TCP/IP and Open System Interconnection (OSI) telecommunications standards, Z39.50 for client-server based information retrieval systems, Z39.58 for the common command language, standards for an ILL protocol, and a number of others in more specialized areas.

REFERENCES

Baker, Shirley K., and Mary E. Jackson. 1992. *Maximizing Access, Minimizing Cost: A First Step Toward the Information Access Future*. Washington, DC: Association of Research Libraries.

Balas, Janet L. 1993. "OPACs and Much More." *Computers in Libraries* 13(1): 28+.

Bryn, Geffert. 1993. "Community Networks in Libraries: A Case Study of the Freenet P.A.T.H." *Public Libraries* 32: 91+.

Engle, Mary E., Marilyn Lutz, William W. Jones, Jr., and Genevieve E. Engel. 1993. *Internet Connections: A Librarian's Guide to Dial-up Access and Use*. Chicago: American Library Association.

Getz, Malcom. "Document Delivery." 1991. *The Bottom Line* 5(4): 40–44.

Gilster, Paul. 1993. *The Internet Navigator*. New York: John Wiley & Sons.

Jackson, Mary E. 1993. *North American Interlibrary Loan/Document Delivery Project: ILL/DD Management System Description*. Washington, DC: Association of Research Libraries.

Krol, Ed. 1992. *The Whole Internet: User's Guide & Catalog*. Sebastopol, CA: O'Reilly & Associates.

Lane, Elizabeth, and Craig Summerhill. 1993. *Internet Primer for Information Professionals*. Westport, CT: Meckler.

Leach, Ronald G. 1993. "Electronic Document Delivery: New Options for Libraries." *The Journal of Academic Librarianship* 18(6): 359–364.

Machovec, George S. 1989. "Locally Loaded Databases in Arizona State University's Online Catalog Using the CARL System." *Information Technology and Libraries* 8(2): 161–171.

Machovec, George S. 1990. "The NPTN and the Cleveland Free-Net Community Computer System." *Online Libraries and Microcomputers* 8(11): 1–4.

Machovec, George S. 1993. *Telecommunications, Networking and Internet Glossary.*
    Chicago: American Library Association.

Potter, William Gray. 1989. "Expanding the Online Catalog." *Information Technology
    and Libraries* 8(2): 99–104.

Sloan, Bernard G. 1991. *Linked Systems for Resource Sharing.* Boston, MA: G.K. Hall
    & Co.

Turner, Fay. 1990. "The Interlibrary Loan Protocol: An OSI Solution to ILL Messaging."
    Library Hi Tech. Issue 32: 73–82.

Wessling, Julie. 1992. "Document Delivery: A Primary Service for the Nineties."
    Advances in Librarianship, 16: 1–31.

2 Implications of New and Emerging Technologies on Reference Service

Johannah Sherrer

Libraries, like other societal institutions, are being affected by two external forces: changes in technology and changes in demand. Due to the exponential growth of new and emerging technologies, these can no longer be considered simple evolutionary changes. Continual technological advances are changing public demand for goods and services worldwide, and libraries, like other institutions, appear to be grappling with how to successfully manage this change. In fact, a whole genre of library literature on managing change has come into being along with its own group of experts and consultants. The idea of managing change, however, is a tame one compared to the challenge of reforming totally how we staff, budget, theorize, and deliver information in reference services. Those who are attempting to integrate emerging technologies into reference services are primarily concerned with how new technologies affect staff and library services. Rarely are reference departments integrating the changes in patron demand into service options.

TRENDS IN NEW AND EMERGING TECHNOLOGIES

Rather than identify the actual trends in new technologies being covered in other chapters, the effort here is to characterize them as they relate to the delivery of reference services. The first characterization is that emerging technologies are by their nature in stark conflict with existing library methodology, which is designed to manage the still dominant format of print media. Second, new technologies provide access during times that the traditional library is closed or when staff are not available. Third, fewer protocols are required to get to the information as compared to the complexities of human-to-human transactions. Fourth, database commands are increasingly transparent, whereas the definition and composition of databases are often masked. Fifth, there are times when it appears to many reference librarians that the added value of speed, ease of use, and sheer increase of mass, are replacing quality, control, and selectivity.

Much of this dichotomy exists not only because new technologies are designed and geared for the end-user but also because they are marketed to reach the masses. Rather than complementing existing reference services, most new technologies are smashing right through them not withstanding the efforts of reference librarians to control or harness their use and, sometimes, even their availability.

IMPLICATION FOR THE PHILOSOPHY OF SERVICE

Calvin Mooers states that "a new technology is composed of two parts: a new kind of physical device and a new philosophy or method for using it. The one generally cannot be used without the other" (1976: 18). The dichotomy that can exist between existing reference processes as new technologies emerge can cause confusion or apparent contradictions in the stated or implied philosophy of service. Despite advances in technology, much of the basis for existing service philosophies is building-based rather than network-based; based on staff mediation rather than end-user independence; fixated on cost rather than suitability; and in most cases, place value decisions in the hands of the profession rather than the end-user.

It is often assumed that reference service in public libraries is different from that offered in college and university libraries and that both of these are quite different from the type of service offered in special libraries. New and emerging technologies are blurring these distinctions as the same type of products are being successfully marketed to what used to be considered dissimilar needs and groups. Are new technologies changing the philosophy of reference services? If they are not, they should be. The number of users is increasing, patron comfort with technology is increasing, and users are demanding that information be delivered on their own terms. Whether or not reference librarians approve it, it is ultimately the responsibility of the patron to select not only appropriate databases but specific articles as well. This does not mean that assistance or consultation is not provided. We must, however, begin to suspend generalized judgments on the effectiveness of a database or the overall quality of journal or magazine. We must create an open exchange on the merits of a particular source as it applies to a particular situation. If we fail to consider these factors in a revision of service philosophy, the commercial sector will make the decisions for us by relegating to reference departments the information needs of those who have yet to be reached by commercial sources.

Clearly, new and emerging technologies are changing traditional patron/staff interaction. How can it be otherwise? How can technology be changing access for users as dramatically as it is and not be changing access just as dramatically for information providers? A perusal of the professional literature suggests that new technologies are creating more stress in significant proportions for staff while simultaneously delighting users, increasing use of information services, and adding a new level of user pleasure and success not previously experienced. The technologies outlined in the preceding chapter are challenging the success of traditional reference methodology and process. As a profession we are responding so slowly and cautiously that many reference librarians find themselves out of touch with the "virtual reality" of their users.

The exercise of defining user characteristics becomes problematic when libraries are providing services and databases for an unseen public. Libraries still define their users based on formal constituencies and the providers of library budgets. But most users think of libraries in a more generic sense without user restrictions or content limitations. Electronic library users share these characteristics, too. Users who mine the Internet for information have little regard for institutional contributions to this largely uncharted mass of data, which is open and free to anyone with the equipment, curiosity, and stamina to delve into the contents.

IMPACT ON STAFF AND STAFFING LEVELS

The key to understanding and incorporating new technologies into reference services is to concentrate on "new" rather than "technologies." Successful implementation depends on staff attitude toward incorporating change, any kind of change, into existing operations. One strategy is to focus on the similarities between the new product or technological application and existing services. Although this is a non-threatening starting point, it must be regarded as just the beginning of the analysis, and not the key factor in determining how the innovation will be integrated into existing services. It is more critical to note what is unique in the product rather than the similarities. Although similarities may serve as a hook for staff understanding, it is a mistake to assume that users have that same frame of reference or that they can appreciate the specialized analogy so apparent to reference staff. As long as reference personnel continue to relate to new technologies from the traditional frame of reference they will continue to miss the true impact of the innovation. Alexander Graham Bell invented the telephone in 1876. Yet how many reference departments today still give preference to the walk-in patron over telephone reference? Is it beneficial to use one of the oldest forms of technology, the telephone, only for local or personal calls rather than calling government and private agencies for statistical data or other specific forms of information? And, when the telephone is used to deliver information, how often is it a last recourse or a "special" case?

Along those same lines, is it beneficial or strategic to use technology only after we have exhausted print sources? Is it strategic to use fax technology, for example, only on rush occasions? Is it plausible to continue in the mode of simply steering users to general sources or possibilities rather than providing or working with the patron until specific answers are found? We need to reevaluate reference services in the light of user expectations for information. We need to relinquish protocol, control, and process and focus only on user need and what is necessary to fulfill that need. Large percentages of library budgets need to be reallocated to new and emerging technologies. Our track record indicates that we operate on the belief that these technologies are for future implementation rather than the present, and that adopting a wait-and-see attitude is prudent budgetary rationale. Every reference department in every shape, size, and type of library today must be thinking of new and emerging technologies as part of everyday business.

Technology does and will continue to influence staffing levels. In many cases, technology eliminates or reduces the skill level of a position. In many instances, new technologies introduce new types of skills and training requirements that may or may not involve the acquisition of a masters in library science. New technologies are requiring that reference departments reevaluate hours of operation, staffing levels, the degree of specialization, relationships with other types of libraries, other internal library departments, and the assumptions underlying institutional uniqueness.

IMPACT ON REFERENCE QUESTIONS

Reference librarians commonly refer to several types of reference transactions: general bibliographic assistance; specific factual questions; and directional, and recently, technical assistance. General bibliographic assistance refers to questions similar to the following: "I'm writing a paper on the practice of medicine during the Civil War" or "I'm thinking about remodeling my kitchen, where are your do-it-yourself books?" In each of these cases, technology allows patrons to peruse databases electronically to further refine their topics or just browse among entries in a very broad manner. The role of the reference librarian is to explain the mechanical steps of searching electronically and to offer assistance or options in framing the query. Too often, librarians remain in the 1970s mode of the precise searcher, and consequently address the query in a closed, narrowly focused manner rather than explore electronic options with the patron. Librarians often assume that the initial request for assistance is license for a prescribed lecture on generic searching techniques and a tacit request for assistance from an information expert on general searching strategies. It is firmly believed by many reference librarians that the patron, who has a specific information need, is actually absorbing the mini-Bl session and then translating it into the necessary steps needed to isolate the particular information need. In this case, the librarian is demonstrating his or her expertness rather than limiting his or her potential to the level necessary to provide the information.

Reference librarians can now answer many more factual questions because of advances in technology. In the past, it was not uncommon for reference librarians to find specific information by browsing through a text or refer the patron to a title related to the topic so that the user could search for the specific information. Librarians need to realize that specific answers can be provided to many more questions by searching abstract contents or full text sources. Information retrieval and the searching capabilities that accompany it are slowly, steadily, and surely shifting emphasis from the book or article as a whole to paragraphs or maybe even single sentences. Yet there seems to be a reluctance to search online for specific facts. Online searching can be quicker for verifications of name spelling, geographical references, biographical and factual data, specific dates, legislative progress on a bill, and various statistical data, yet most reference librarians first check print sources and then often go further only at the insistence of the user. Reference staff should be thinking about how new technology is changing the way questions are answered as well as the type of question that is being asked. Are more general bibliographical queries being handled without staff mediation as a result of end-user searching queries? Are reference print collections shrinking? How do we define a successful reference transaction? How do patrons define a successful reference encounter? Is the nature of reference work changing fundamentally? These are examples of the kind of questions that should be addressed as we incorporate emerging technologies into reference services.

Technical assistance refers to almost any problem with a printer, a frozen screen, and, in many cases, simple startup instructions for the novice user. Unfortunately, this area is dominating the scene in terms of new visions for reference services. New ideas for desk staffing, training, service hours, and the utilization of professional librarians are influenced predominately by in-house patron use of technology. Articles are being written about the efficacy of maintaining a reference desk or private offices or both (Massey-Burzio 1992; Ford 1986). Articles appear on new roles for librarians and support staff based on anecdotal experiences or efforts to remove the professional staff from technical assistance queries (Oberg 1992; Campbell 1992; Massey-Burzio 1992). Reference departments are reorganizing and adding staff to save professional librarians from the tedium of technical assistance queries. The preoccupation with technical issues at this level is missing the point. Reference librarians need to be asking themselves harder questions. Is technology influencing information-seeking behavior of information providers? Are we able to answer questions that went unanswered in the past? Are we investigating the substantive aspects of information delivery? Much remains to be done that will link the experiences of librarians to those of the user. Now, more than ever, it is imperative that problem solving in reference services be patron based rather than framed in a managerial context of organizational theory.

Reference departments that set up artificial boundaries that limit the extent of their involvement in providing information will find themselves backed into a corner with little or no room for continued development. New technologies are forcing reference departments to go well beyond the walls of the building and to demand knowledge of tools not owned but searchable and usable in an electronic format. Libraries that can not afford annual subscriptions to the citation indexes, for example, can search them online. The issue is that most reference departments still organize themselves around their "bought and paid for" print collection. So, even when sources are available online, the likelihood of their being consulted as freely as the print counterpart is often related to whether or not it was ever owned or held in the print format. Too often, reference librarians structure their query decisions and actual practice of the reference art on the limitations of print acquisitions. The new technologies described in the preceding chapter should be forcing all of us into a new mode of reference service, one without walls, one without bibliographic penalty, and one that stretches each practicing librarian to new daily levels of personal achievement.

It is time for reference services to move beyond bibliographic access toward actual document delivery by accepting responsibility for providing both documents and information. This should mean actually securing documents, through locating the exact information requested and retrieving it simultaneously. In this manner, the reference librarian assumes a larger role in the general collection development decisions instead of automatically sending the patron to the interlibrary loan office.

IMPLICATIONS FOR BUDGETS

The budgeting implications of incorporating new technologies are often accompanied by the notion that anything new requires new moneys or additional dollars. Until librarians acknowledge that financing the "new" is the norm rather than the exception, the implementation and full utilization of emerging technologies will be hampered. Traditional patterns of allocation will have to change to establish opportunities for new or enhanced services as priorities. Fees for consortia membership, staff training, equipment, public relations, and marketing strategies are all significantly more important than ever before. Reallocation will affect total library operational dollars not just reference activities or collection development. New and emerging technologies are reorienting entire library operations toward users more comprehensively than ever before. Libraries now exist for the user at hand and the ability of a library to support strong reference services constitute a library's worth in a way that collection building never has. The notion of core collections, and almost every assumption that has gone into collection building in the past when considering budgeting reallocations must be questioned. This premise is one that holds true for both large and small libraries. New technologies are challenging traditional library categories previously held in check by an environment defined by collection size, staff size, and the magnitude of sheer square footage. Now small libraries can operate and provide services at par with larger institutions. Distinctions exist as to levels of service, but service is defined by "attitude" as well as by budget. Although staff may feel they have little control over the budget, they do control the attitude that creates and supports library services.

PRACTICAL STRATEGIES FOR INCORPORATING NEW AND EMERGING TECHNOLOGIES INTO REFERENCE SERVICES

Practical strategies for incorporating new and emerging technologies into reference services require the "stuff" of which good, solid reference professionals are made. That "stuff" is solid knowledge of the sources;

not just presently available titles, but a working knowledge of the history of how information is organized, classified, and disseminated. Second, the ability to work within the framework of possibility, with an emphasis on what a new source brings to the whole rather than a detailed critical analysis that judges the work in isolation is imperative. Third, we must eliminate the mindset that because sources can be approached and explored independently, librarians must save the general public from the misuse of tools. Fourth, and now more than ever, the emphasis must be on answering the question, not building a core of key works for possible use in the future. Fifth, reference responsibility does not stop with the exhaustion of local sources. Sixth, we must strive to provide the specific information requested as opposed to referring the patron to other sources or libraries.

Intellectually, the mind of the reference librarian must be willing to search the universe of available knowledge and focus on meeting the patron's need as completely as possible. The added value the reference librarian brings to information delivery in a technological environment is commitment to service with all the personal tenacity that true commitment requires. This involves genuine curiosity, an interest in people and human communication, and the desire to improve individual performance and levels of achievement.

Libraries, specifically reference services, are experiencing a major challenge to traditional practice. Commercial information vendors are successfully marketing user-oriented information systems to the general public. The commercial orientation is customer based, becoming more and more economical, and, unlike library services, the vendors are designing goods and services according to customer preference. Vendors are not mission based unless increased sales are considered a company prerogative. Most libraries are so mission based that occasionally the stated mission becomes more important than meeting client needs and preferences. Library staff lose sight of the fact that it is users we are serving rather than the mission. Technological advances are often the responsibility of only one or two department members and others are slow to incorporate emerging technologies into the mental processes that eventually define the scope of library services and materials.

Practical strategies for incorporating new technologies and assessing their implications include the following:

Revamp budgeting priorities. Do not wait for special funding to incorporate emerging technologies into reference services. Reallocate funding from within traditional budget lines. Waiting for special allocations or grants often compromises the advantage of adding new services. Changes in technology are so much a part of everyday library practices that to fail to incorporate such change is counterproductive to the delivery of solid reference services. It is important to lobby continually for flexible budgeting and creative funding strategies and to sacrifice existing services for the opportunity to introduce new ideas and concepts. It is not reasonable to expect to continue handling business as usual while incorporating new and emerging technologies.

Eliminate services with lower demand. We often continue to offer a particular service because we have become accustomed to the familiarity of it and have finally reached the point of being able to anticipate problems. Our control of the quality of the service is established, our control of the needed staffing and funding is maintained, and our training manuals and policies are complete. The idea of elimination or drastic reduction contradicts efficient management techniques. The true contradiction to efficient management is to maintain services of low use when they can be duplicated electronically.

Give all staff responsibility for incorporating new technologies into reference activities. Too common today is the notion that those with an interest in computers can handle the introduction of new products and the maintenance of computer related services. Also common is the idea that new processes require new personnel or "new blood." And last, but not least, is the organizational response that creates and advertises new positions for a "CD-ROM Librarian" or "Electronic Services Librarian" or even an "Internet Librarian." It is not possible to continue offering appropriate reference services by failing to incorporate existing staff into the problems and issues associated with the exponential growth of new and emerging technologies.

Allocate time and money for staff training and development. Dollars and time need to be devoted to staff training and development. It is time to place the "coping with change" workshops on the back burner and replace them with real training opportunities either on- or off-site. It is time to upgrade staff abilities by providing them with current state-of-the-art equipment that will encourage creative and productive uses of technology. It is time for library managers to raise their expectations of staff performance through appropriate support.

Reflect on change. It is also important to provide time for reflection on change. Although there are organizations that proceed cautiously in adding expensive and unknown technologies, there are also those organizations that proceed full speed ahead. In both cases, the necessity to reflect on the full importance of what they have or have not been doing needs to be addressed.

Commit to service on the patron's terms. It is necessary to keep in mind that the user may be as savvy as we are regarding information opportunities; that they may own quality computer hardware; that they have experience with computer applications either from their jobs, schools, or other service organizations; and that they are the best judges of what works well for them and what most satisfies their information needs.

Communicate with colleagues as well as with patrons. Reference librarians develop strong interpersonal skills for dealing with the public, but often fail to use those same skills when dealing with their reference colleagues. The rate of change of information technology is so great that the combined task of staying informed while delivering informed service requires almost constant communication with colleagues. It is not unusual for reference personnel to adhere to one set of communication standards for working with the public and operate internally with quite another set of values and expectations.

Constantly challenge the status quo. Always keep looking for the better mousetrap. It is one thing to be critical and/or evaluative, but to do so without actively seeking alternative strategies is often self-defeating.

Develop comfort with change and being imprecise. Technology is changing libraries in general and reference in particular. The professional literature is full of articles dealing with change, anticipating the future and staff reorganization. It is clear that reference departments that are comfortable with change and operate in an environment that is imprecise, succeed in advancing services while others falter.

Reward flexibility and new ideas. We all need to appreciate flexibility in our peers and colleagues. However, for the most part, traditional library management rewards structure and merely takes advantage of personnel flexibility. This is not just a management issue. We all need to appreciate and support new ideas from colleagues. As the originators of new ideas, we need to recognize that the flexibility and openness of our colleagues brings new ideas to fruition.

Think, talk, and write about the future. We all find time to complain about the present, and we should find just as much time to think freely and creatively about the future. It is a good idea to step back and try to envision where we were, where we are, and where we can be. This should be done individually and collectively.

Seek out colleagues from other institutions for ideas and a frame of reference. Although libraries have individual differences, there is much they have in common. It is beneficial to seek out colleagues from other institutions for ideas, or just a frame of reference. Library personnel are fortunate in that many opportunities exist for collaborative efforts and formal or informal networking. Maintaining a frame of reference during periods of rapid change is beneficial for positive growth and advancement.

Look to other professions for solutions and problem solving. There are practical opportunities to be gained by studying problem-solving efforts from other professions. Customer service strategies from business, instructional technology from schools and colleges, and inventory management or public relations from industries can all serve as catalysts for problem solving in the delivery of information services. But even more specifically, we should be studying our direct commercial counterparts such as document delivery businesses and online vendors, such as Prodigy or America Online.

CONCLUSION

Calvin Mooers' statement made in 1976 regarding new technologies is the key to successfully incorporating emerging technologies into reference services. In an article titled "Technology of Information Handling—A Pioneer's View," which appeared in the *Bulletin of the American Society for Information Science* in March of 1976, Mooers states that a new technology is made up of two parts. One is the physical device itself and the other is, or should be, a new philosophy or method for using it. He further states that the one usually cannot be used without the other. Reference librarians need to routinely consider this idea when integrating technologies into daily practices. Mooers' comment also contributes to the notion that librarians need to work with the originators of new technologies and supply the new philosophy or application that will improve information dissemination.

It is disconcerting for many reference librarians that the public appears to be seeking information from sources other than libraries and that this public feels confident that they are getting what they need. Reference librarians need to recognize that not only is this happening, but that it may be beneficial. In the end, it is the user who determines the relevance of the information found. The fact that information is readily sought from sources outside of libraries is an indication that our delivery methods and service policies should be examined. It is evident that we can learn not only from information consumers, our users, but also from our commercial competitors.

The following is a timetable in progress. It is a personal (the author's) charting of information technology as it relates to reference services. It is a subjective selection that represents only one element of Calvin Mooers' formula for the successful utilization of emerging technologies. It can, however, serve as stimulus for the analysis of reference services in the context of new technologies. This chart is a starting point for dialogue and at some point should include the all important second element of Mooers' formula.

TIMETABLE OF INFORMATION HANDLING—DEVICES, USES, EVENTS

The author acknowledges the value and work of two key sources in the compilation of this timetable. First is an article by J. E. Emard (1976: 51–56) that chronicles information science and libraries. The second is *Timetables of Science* (Hellemans 1988). Both of these sources include many more entries than were selected for this particular compilation. In addition, the *World Encyclopedia for Library and Information Services* (Electronic Data Sources 1993) and *A Century of Library Service: Librarianship in the United States and Canada* (Jackson, Herling, and Josey 1976) were very helpful. A history of computers and computing appears annually in the *Computer Industry Almanac*.

1791	Yale University publishes the first library catalog subdivided by subject classes
1828	Noah Webster compiles the first comprehensive American dictionary
1834	Charles Babbage designs the "Analytical Engine," the first general-purpose computer
1839	John Dancer combines photography with microscopy to produce the first microphotograph
1844	Samuel F. B. Morse sends the first public telegraph message
1848	William F. Poole, assisted by fellow librarians, begins the *Index to Periodical Literature*
1854	Boston Public Library is opened, the first "modern public library" in the United States
1868	Christopher Sholes, Carlos Glidden, and S. W. Soule produce the first practical typewriter
1875	The first typewritten book manuscript is the manuscript of *The Adventures of Tom Sawyer*, by Mark Twain. It is typed on a Remington typewriter in 1875. *Life on the Mississippi* is also typewritten the same year. Mark Twain does not publicize these

facts, as he does not want to write testimonials or explain the operation of the machine to inquirers

1876	The American Library Association (ALA) is founded
	Melvil Dewey devises the Dewey Decimal Classification System
	Charles A. Cutter publishes rules for dictionary catalogs
	Alexander Graham Bell invents the telephone
	Thomas Alva Edison invents the mimeograph
1878	Thomas Alva Edison secures a patent for the phonograph
1884	Herman Hollerith of the U.S. Census Bureau develops tabulating machine for use with punched cards to facilitate 1890 census
	First successful fountain pen is invented by Lewis Waterman
1891	The Library Bureau introduces card cabinets made to hold one row of cards in each drawer. These drawers can be removed from the cabinet and placed on a table for consultation. Previous cabinets held two rows of cards in each drawer and could not be removed from the cabinet
1892	Telephone connection between Chicago and New York is made
	The Library Bureau claims to have developed the vertical file. One made by the bureau is displayed at the Chicago World's Fair
1893	The Library Bureau begins a cooperative cataloging service. In 1896 the Library Bureau transfers the responsibility for cooperative cataloging to the publishing section of the American Library Association, but continues to manufacture, print, and supply cards to subscribers. When the Library of Congress makes its catalog cards available in 1901 it is no longer necessary for the American Library Association or the Library Bureau to continue their cooperative cataloging efforts
	ALA Index begins
1899	Magnetic-tape recorder invented
1902	Printed catalog card distribution program begun by the Library of Congress
	Guide to the Study and Use of Reference Books published, later published as the *Guide to Reference Books*
1904	The Library of Congress publishes its classification system in outline form
1908	The Anglo-American cataloging rules are published
1911	The Computing Tabulating Recordings Company, later to become IBM Corporation, begins operation

1918	World's first airmail service is established between New York, Philadelphia, and Washington, D.C.
1922	The Library Bureau begins to market the Russell Index, a system for filing public records. The purpose of the system was to bring together in one file names that sounded the same, but were spelled differently
1924	First use of facsimile transmission takes place between Cleveland and New York and is printed in the *New York Times*
1925	Charles Jenkins invents the television
1926	National Interlibrary Code is adopted in the United States
	First successful scheduled airline in the United States begins operations
1930	Vannevar Bush develops the analog machine that electromechanically uses gears powered by electricity
	Ralph Parker conceives the idea of using punched-card equipment for library circulation work
	Gaylord Brothers introduce their electric automatic charging machine
1934	The American Federation for the blind produces the first talking books
	University of Texas Library introduces a circulation system using punched cards
1935	Publishers and scholars work out an uneasy truce called the "Gentlemen's Agreement" whereby it is understood that the reproduction of single copies for the sole use of a researcher is permissible
1936	Konrad Zuse builds primitive form of digital computer using electromagnetic relays instead of tubes (or transistors)
1937	American law student Chester Carlson invents xerography, the first method of photocopying
	The American Documentation Institute is formed. By 1950 it becomes the focal point for technological research in the application of computers to library procedures
late 1930s	Photo-offset lithography eliminates the need for laborious typesetting opening the doors to a vast reprint market
1943	A team headed by Alan Turing develops Colossus, the first all-electronic calculating device (it uses vacuum tubes); unlike a general-purpose computer, however, Colossus is dedicated to cracking German codes—and is very good at it, possibly influencing the course of World War II

1944	The second electronic digital computer, the Automatic Sequence Controlled Calculator, or Mark I, is completed by Howard Aiken and a team of engineers from IBM: it uses punched paper tape for programming and vacuum tubes to calculate problems, but breaks down frequently from problems with vacuum tubes
	Vannevar Bush advances the idea of a "Memex" machine that would store books and journals on spools of film and select and provide individual copies on demand through electronic processing
1945	Ralph Shaw builds a prototype of "Memex" called the "Bush Rapid Selector"
	John von Neumann publishes his *First Draft of Report on the EDVAC*, placing the concept of the EDVAC (Electronic Discrete Variable Computer) in the public domain
1946	John William Mauchly and John Prosper Eckert complete ENIAC, the first all-purpose, all-electronic computer; it does not use binary numerals, but has vacuum tubes arranged to display decimal numerals; it draws so much electricity that it causes the lights in a nearby town to dim each time it is used
1948	Manchester University's Mark 1 prototype, a stored-program electronic computer starts operating; legend has it that a moth gets into the circuitry causing it to malfunction; because of this event, the term "bug" is coined to describe all computer malfunctions
	Hungarian-American physicist Peter Mark Goldmark develops the first long-playing record in the United States
	English-American physicist William Bradford Shockley, American physicist Walter Houser Brattain, and American physicist John Bardeen discover the transistor, a tiny device that works like a vacuum tube but uses less power
1950	The "Berkner Report" advises the U.S. State Department on science, foreign relations, and the national flow of sci/tech information
1951	John William Mauchly and John Prosper Eckert build UNIVAC I, the first electronic computer to be commercially available and the first to store data on magnetic tape; it is sold by Remington Rand
	Computers and Automation, the first journal devoted exclusively to computing, begins publication on a regular basis
	The National Microfilm Association begins
1951–1956	Development and refinement of magnetic tapes and disks as a means of memory storage

1952   The CBS television network uses a UNIVAC computer to predict
          the results of the U.S. presidential election; UNIVAC's first pre-
          diction of a landslide is right on the mark but not believed by its
          operators; they quickly reprogram it so that it incorrectly predicts
          a close contest

1953   American physicist Charles Hard Townes develops the maser, the
          precursor of the laser

          Mortimer Taube and associates introduce the uniterm system of
          coordinate indexing

1954   UNIVAC I becomes commercially available

          Bibliographic searching via computer is demonstrated in the form
          of batch searching

          Optical scanners are introduced

1955   The first optical fibers are produced by Narinder Kapary in London

          The IBM 650 becomes commercially available

          The first "supercomputer" NORC (Naval Ordinance Research Cal-
          culator) is delivered to the U.S. Naval Weapons Laboratory

1956   John Backus and a team at IBM invent FORTRAN, the first
          computer programming language; previously, computer programs
          had to be installed in machine language

          Stanislaw Ulam programs a computer to play chess on a 6×6 board;
          the program called MANIAC I, becomes the first computer pro-
          gram to beat a human in a game

1957   Columbia University physics graduate student Gordon Gould on
          November 11 has the idea that will translate into the laser; Gould
          does not, however, apply for a patent until 1959; by then others
          have also begun work on lasers; Gould's patent claims are not
          accepted until after 1986

          Reference Services Division of ALA comes into being under the
          leadership of Louis Shores

1958   Hans Peter Luhn devises a computer program for automatic index-
          ing and abstracting

1959   The first commercial Xerox copier is introduced

          Grace Murray Hopper invents COBOL, a computer language de-
          signed for business uses

1960   Microfiche technology begins

          Theodore Harold Maimen develops the first laser in May using a
          ruby cylinder

          Protosynthex allows access to the full *Golden Book Encyclopedia*
          with proximity term searching

1961	Roger Summit of Lockheed Missiles and Space Corporation demonstrates the ability to search an in-house database from the Lockheed Library
	The Massachusetts Institute of Technology (MIT) develops the first time-sharing computer
	RQ begins publication
1962	The Aviation Supply Office in Philadelphia introduces time-sharing on its computer for inventory control
	Roger Summit creates the DIALOG retrieval language
1963	The minicomputer is introduced by Digital Equipment Corp.
1964	Permanent press clothing is introduced
	Picturephone service is developed and operated on a trial basis in Chicago, New York, and Washington, D.C.
	Touch tone telephone buttons replace rotary dials
	McLuhan's *Understanding Media* is published
	The Library of Congress acquires its first computer and commissions a study to determine how machine readable catalog records could be produced and used
	MEDLARS (Medical Literature Analysis and Retrieval System) is made available to the general publish as a batch retrospective search service
	The Medical Library Association (MLA) Continuing Education Committee offers two courses at the annual MLA meeting: one is titled "Basic Punched Card Principles for Librarians" and the other is "Implications of Machines in Medical Libraries"
	RQ carries two articles under the titles, "Goodbye Reference Librarian!" and "Are Reference Librarians Obsolete?"
1965	John Kemeny and Thomas Kurtz develop BASIC (beginners all-purpose symbolic instruction code), a computer language for beginners; it becomes the main programming language used by owners of personal computers, although most commercial programs for personal computers are in more sophisticated languages
	First commercial communications satellite, Early Bird, is placed in orbit
mid-1960s	Third-generation computers, using integrated circuits, miniaturization, system logic improvements, and higher speeds, come into being
1966	MARC (Machine Readable Cataloging) program initiated at the Library of Congress

American Chemical Society issues first journal to be published by computer composition (Journal of Chemical Documents V. 6)

A survey by the Special Libraries Association reveals that 209 libraries are using data processing equipment principally for serials management and acquisitions. The survey cites 131 installations using data processing equipment in reference work or document retrieval: 76 in special libraries in industrial settings; 18 in colleges; and none are reported in public libraries

ERIC (Educational Resources Information Center), a network of clearinghouses is formed to index, abstract, and distribute microfiche

1967   OCLC is incorporated as a not-for-profit corporation

Washington State Library accepts responsibility for developing a system to provide shared bibliographic support

Later becomes WLN

1968   MIT starts INTREX to test applications of the computer for information retrieval by automating its engineering library

1969   "Bubble memory" devices are created to use in computers; unlike conventional memory devices, bubble memory continues to remember even when the computer is turned off

Carlos Cuadra predicts the role of the library as an information provider will slip into other hands should libraries fail to assume a leadership role

1970   The floppy disk is introduced for storing data used by computers

MEDLINE (MEDLARS On-line) of the National Library of Medicine begins

1971   Direct telephone dialing, as opposed to operator-assisted calling, begins between parts of the United States and Europe on a regular basis

The first microprocessor, now known as the chip, is introduced by Intel in the United States

The American National Standards Institute (ANSI) approves MARCII as a national standard

OCLC begins operations in Ohio

Niklaus Wirth develops Pascal (named for Blaise Pascal who invented the first calculator), a popular language used on home computers

1972   Computers are applied to the functions of the U.S. court system (indexing, docketing, information gathering)

The National Library of Medicine (NLM) utilizes TYMNET, the first public communications network for access to MEDLINE

OCLC begins to operate interstate

ARPANET, the experimental coast-to-coast network of computers developed by the U.S. Department of Defense Department becomes operational (Emard); it is the precursor of the Internet

Dialog Information Services begins operation as a vendor of on-line bibliographic services

New Yorks Times Information Bank offers limited computer access to its columns for its own staff

1973	Mead Data introduces LEXIS, a full text online information service of primary sources in law and legal research
	Computer-coded labels are introduced in supermarkets
1974	*Radio-Electronics* publishes an article describing the construction of a "personal computer"
	Dow Jones New Retrieval begins as a stock-quote service for brokers and offers current and historical stock averages, foreign exchange trends, and earnings forecasts for U.S. companies
	Research Libraries Group (RLG) formed
1975	The first personal computer, the Altair 8800, is introduced in kit form in the United States; it has 256 bytes of memory
	Byte, the first computer magazine begins publication
	The first computer store opens in Santa Monica, California
1976	IBM develops the ink-jet printer
	BRS (Bibliographic Retrieval Services, Inc.) begins providing commercial online services; the entry of BRS into the online services field revolutionizes the pricing structure as other firms quickly lower to become competitive
1977	The Apple II, the first personal computer available in assembled form and the first to be truly successful, is introduced; the Apple II is also the first personal computer with color graphics capability
1978	Apple brings out the first disk drive for use with personal computers
	Epson introduces the dot-matrix printer for personal computers
	Total computer use in the United States exceeds a half a million units
1979	Visicalc introduces the first spreadsheet program for personal computers; this enables personal computer users to develop business applications without learning to program a computer
	OCLC's Interlibrary Loan Subsystem becomes operational
	Philips and Sony Corporations agree on a common standard for the new compact disk digital audio system

1980   Mead Data introduces NEXIS, a full text information service for
              news and current events

              CAS (Chemical Abstracts Service) introduces CAS Online

              InfoWorld begins publication

              Total computers in use in the United States exceeds one million

1981   The IBM personal computer, using what is to become an industry-
              standard disk operating system (DOS), is introduced

              NOTIS begins making its online catalog software commercially
              available

1982   Compact disk players are introduced

              BRS and DIALOG introduce flat rate simplified versions of their
              more popular databases for home searchers; these services, BRS
              AFTERDARK and DIALOG's KNOWLEDGE INDEX are avail-
              able in the evenings and on weekends.

              Compaq brings out the first "clone" of the IBM personal computer,
              a computer that uses the same operating system as the IBM PC and
              that has other elements in common so that most IBM programs can
              be used

              Epson's HX-20 becomes the first laptop computer

              Time Magazine names the computer its "Man of the Year"

1983   Apple's Lisa brings the mouse and pulldown menus to the personal
              computer; a mouse is a device that moves the cursor on the screen
              as a result of moving the mouse on a hard surface; pressing a button
              on the mouse sends a command to the computer, depending on
              where the cursor is located

              BRS offers the full text of 32 medical journals

              Lotus 1-2-3 spreadsheet program is launched

              Gateway software appears in the library marketplace; it is used
              with microcomputers serving as terminals for database searching

              Federal court Judge Harold S. Greene issues his historic ruling that
              dismantles AT&T's telecommunications monopoly

              Total computers in use in the United States exceed 10 million units

1984   Optical disks for the storage of computer data are introduced

              IBM introduces a megabit random-access memory (RAM) chip
              with four times the memory of earlier chips

              Apple brings Lisa technology down to an affordable price with its
              instantly popular Macintosh computer

              WILSONLINE inaugurated

EASYNET introduces a menu driven service for easy searching of BRS, DIALOG, SDC, VU-TEXT, and other online services; it features options for users with no previous knowledge of online searching

IBM's PC AT is the first personal computer to use a new chip to expand speed and memory in an existing personal computer architecture

1985 Infotrac, a video disk product from IAC, provides access to millions of articles citations; it becomes the first mass-market laser disk success story and revolutionizes end user searching

AT&T Bell Laboratories achieves the equivalent of sending 300,000 simultaneous telephone conversations or 200 high-resolution television channels at once over a single optical fiber

The Apple LaserWriter laser printer opens up the desktop publishing area

1986 Compaq leaps past IBM by introducing computers using an advanced 32-bit chip, the Intel 80386

Total computers in use in the United States exceed 30 million

1987 Apple's Macintosh II and Macintosh SE become the most powerful personal computers available

IBM brings out the Personal System/2 group of personal computers, based on 3.5-inch disk drives, hard disks, enhanced graphics, and access to a new operating system that enables interconnections between computers

International Standards Organization (ISO) ratifies the High Sierra standards for CD-ROMs

1988 John L. Gustafson, Gary R. Montry, Robert E. Benner, and coworkers find a way to rewrite problems for computer parallel processing that speeds their solution by a factor of 1000; previously an increase in speed by a factor of 100 was thought to be the limit of this method

Notebook computers, smaller versions of laptops, become popular

Z39.50, a standard protocol for information retrieval is approved by the American National Standards Institute

Collegiate computer hacker (Robert Tappan Morris, Jr.) brings the Internet to national attention when he clogs it with a devious "worm" program

1989 *Information Literacy: Revolution in the Library*, by Breivik and Gee, is published by Macmillan

1990 Mead Data Central offers NEXIS/LEXIS access to educational institutions under subsidized contract arrangements

early 1990s   Tapeloading commercial bibliographic databases into online cata-
              logs becomes popular

              OCLC begins providing general reference to its union catalog
              through EPIC

1991   Clipboard computers appear, replacing the keyboard with a liquid
              crystal screen and electronic stylus

              OCLC field tests FIRSTSEARCH, a gateway service to other major
              bibliographic services as well as its own union catalog

              "Gopher software" developed by a team at the University of Min-
              nesota revolutionizes public access to the Internet

              FIRSTSEARCH offers subscription pricing on three OCLC data-
              bases

              Apple and IBM sign a historic agreement highlighting joint ven-
              tures

              IBM has its first revenue decline in 45 years

1992   Legislation passes creating NREN (the National Research and
              Education Network)

              Microsoft introduces Windows 3.1 and ships nearly 10 million units

              Intel says its next microprocessor will be called Pentium instead of
              586

1993   IBM reports its worst year in history

              Motorola starts shipping the first power PC microprocessor

1994   5,300 databases exist compared to 300 in 1979; there are 2,232
              database producers in 1994 compared to 221 in 1979; and there are
              822 online services compared to 71 in 1979

REFERENCES

Arms, C. (Ed.). 1990. *Campus Strategies for Libraries and Electronic Information.*
     Maynard, MA: Digital Press.
Becker, J. 1984. "An Information Scientist's View on Evolving Information Technol-
     ogy." *Journal of the American Society for Information Science* 35(3): 64–169.
Boulanger, M. 1987. "Online Services at the Reference Desk: New Technologies vs. Old
     Problems." *The Reference Librarian* 15: 269–277.
Boykin, J. F. 1991. "Library Automation 1970–1990: From the Few to the Many."
     Library Administration and Management 5: 10–15.
Bregman, Adeane, and Barbara Mento. 1992. "Reference Roving at Boston College."
     College and Research Libraries News 52 (November): 634–637.
Campbell, Jerry. 1992. "Shaking the Conceptual Foundations of Reference: A Perspec-
     tive." *Reference Services Review* (Winter): 29–36.
Electronic Data Sources. 1993. In *World Encyclopedia of Library and Information
     Services.* Chicago: American Library Association.

Emard, J. E. 1976. "An Information Science Chronology in Perspective." *Bulletin of the American Society for Information Science* 2(8): 51–56.

Ford, Barbara. 1986. "Reference Beyond (And Without) the Reference Desk." *College and Research Libraries* 47 (September): 491–494.

Freeman, M. S. 1991. "Pen, Ink, Keys, and Cards: Some Reflections on Library Technology." *College and Research Libraries* 52(4): 329–335.

Hellemans, A. 1988. *Timetables of Science.* New York: Simon & Schuster.

Higginbotham, Barbara B. 1990. " 'You Only Have to Touch the Keys . . . ': Nineteenth Century Visions of Twentieth Century Technology." *Urban Academic Librarian* 7(2): 40–45.

Jackson, S. L., Herling, E. B., and Josey, E. J. (Eds.). (1976). *A Century of Library Science: Librarianship in the United States and Canada.* Chicago: American Library Association.

Kilgour, F. G. 1987. "Historical Note: A Personalized Prehistory of OCLC." *Journal of the Society for Information Science* 38(5): 381–384.

Massey-Burzio, Virginia. 1992. "Reference Encounters of a Different Kind: A Symposium." *Journal of Academic Librarianship* 18(5): 276–286.

Mooers, C. N. 1976. "Technology of Information Handling—A Pioneer's View." *Bulletin of the American Society for Information Science* 2(8): 18–21.

Oberg, Larry. 1992. "Response to Hammond: Paraprofessionals at the Reference Desk: The End of the Debate." *The Reference Librarian* 37: 105–107.

Pizer, I. H. (1984). "Looking Backward, 1984–1959: Twenty-five Years of Library Automation—A Personal View." *Bulletin of the Medical Library Association* 72(4): 335–348.

Shera, J. H. (1976, March). "Two Centuries of American Librarianship." *Bulletin of the American Society for Information Science* 2(8): 39–40.

Tedd, L. A. (1987, June). "Progress in Documentation—Computer-Based Library Systems: A Review of the Last Twenty-One Years." *Journal of Documentation* 43(2): 145–165.

3 Implications for Bibliographic Instruction

Harvey Sager

Of the many forces that currently impact libraries, the rapid advance and infusion of new information technologies is certainly among the most profound for those of us who provide and promote bibliographic instruction. The impact and influence of emerging technologies on bibliographic instruction (BI) must be understood in context of the evolution of this discipline whose own emergence and growth parallels the computer revolution in libraries.

Although BI as an activity may be as old as the notion of the reference desk itself, the seeds of BI as a library discipline in its own right did not begin to take root until the 1960s. In these early years, computers and libraries were formally introduced through cataloging and record-keeping operations, and library users were kept at a polite distance from library technology. By the late 1970s, user instruction had achieved the momentum of a "movement," with its own leaders, interest groups, language, and literature. This period saw the emergence of COM (Computer Output Microfiche) catalogs, the development and introduction of early on-line catalogs, and the increasing use of librarian-mediated database searching. Although library users came face to face with library automation, most encounters were still chaperoned.

The decade of the 1980s saw the BI movement evolve into a recognized specialization within academic librarianship; it had its own attendant body of research, practical, and scholarly forums, curriculum and its own corps of practicing converts. This was a time of great energy and innovation in libraries. On-line public access catalogs (OPACs) proliferated, and, in many cases, evolved into supercatalogs with access to a variety of information resources including commercial and locally developed databases. With the advent of the OPAC, library instruction programs flourished; instructional departments in academic libraries formed or existing instructional activities were otherwise solidified. Dial-up access to library computers and the emergence of CD-ROM databases placed the power of computing for library research directly in the hands, and in the homes and offices, of library users. End-user applications performed the marriage between BI and technology, and all the libraries' constituencies attended the ceremony.

For BI, this was a decade of growing confidence and influence, as reflected in the many library job announcements requesting instructional experience or interest. Membership and interest in the Association of College and Research Libraries (ACRL) Bibliographic Instruction Section (BIS) soared; this decade saw the formation of the Computer Concerns Committee as a standing committee within BIS, while BIS programs focusing on technology attracted overflow audiences at American Library Association annual conferences. Instructional materials on on-line catalogs and end-user searching flowed into LOEX, the Library Orientation and Exchange Clearinghouse. Information technology was both the subject and the catalyst for a growing body of BI efforts, activities, and research, and BI was still only a little over two decades old. Now, in the decade of the 1990s, we are poised at the edge of a new century, and BI is at a crossroads of reassessment. At the center of this reassessment, too, is the impact of new and emerging information technologies.

If the history of BI is relatively concise, the current boundaries of bibliographic instruction are vast. In the broadest sense, bibliographic instruction, or library user education, might include any and all educational activities planned, designed, and employed to enhance the independent information-gathering and synthesizing skills of information seekers. However, for the purpose of this chapter and to avoid wandering too far afield, this discussion of BI will be limited to those instructional activities that are delivered outside the context of the one-on-one reference desk transaction. Certainly there is a close relationship between BI and traditional reference services, and even a closer relationship between BI and what we often refer to as extended or in-depth reference service or consultation. BI, however, is not a misguided pursuit to make programmatic what can be better accomplished one-on-one at the reference desk; BI and reference services are each distinct and, ideally, complimentary library activities.

A traditional definition of bibliographic instruction might include, but not be limited to, activities such as providing library tours; delivering classroom lectures, presentations, or demonstrations on information gathering skills and resources; developing and teaching credit and non-credit library courses; co-teaching or providing course integrated library instruction; developing print, media, and multimedia library instructional materials; and even creating and implementing library signage systems. Most recently, these activities have been integrated into the broader objectives of creating learning environments that foster critical thinking skills and information literacy. In nearly all of these instructional areas and objectives, new and emerging technologies have provided opportunities, challenges, and impetus. It would not be an exaggeration to say that technology has validated BI as an essential library mission, and revolutionized the "what," the "way," and the "why" we think about, write about, and deliver bibliographic instruction to our diverse user populations.

One of the most significant impacts of technology on BI was not BI's response to technology, but technology's influence on faculty and library administrators' responses to BI. Emerging technologies brought home the importance and necessity of BI to these important constituencies on a scale that sometimes surprised BI's most enthusiastic advocates. Emerging technology was and continues to be an agent for changing attitudes about library user education.

In the early years of BI, before there were end-users, remote users, and Internet explorers, there were only library users. Libraries were conceptualized as real places, not virtual spaces, and our academic library patrons looked and behaved much the same as each preceding generation. Library tours and orientations were the mainstay of BI and, until prodded by technologies that defied our library-based instructional models, BI was primarily source and site based. Librarians emphasized the unique attributes of their favorite library resources, and like real estate salespersons, they professed the credo "location, location, location" as they guided classes through the library. A "This is where . . . " approach shared equal time with a "This is how . . . " approach to library user education. And, a "This is why . . . " approach had not yet found a voice.

This was a time when the Red books (*Library of Congress Subject Headings*) sat with authority on podia near the card catalog like Bibles on a pulpit. The card catalog itself was a library icon and its canyons, often divided by the three familiar access points, suggested the boundaries and organization of both the physical library collection and the intellectual content it described. This was an environment little changed in nearly a half century.

In a user environment that was relatively static, advocates and practitioners of BI often met resistance from faculty who did not perceive or accept librarians as full partners in the educational process. Requests by librarians to conduct class presentations on library resources and research strategies were too often seen by faculty as unnecessary, and as intrusions of dubious value that take away from valuable class time. Efforts on the part of librarians to work collaboratively with faculty to integrate the library into course goals and to improve the effectiveness of library-related research assignments is still, of course, sometimes met with suspicion. After all, in most cases faculty learned how to do library research without such perceived frills, and many are unaware of the gap between their assumptions about students' preparedness to do even basic library research and the reality of these students' library experience and abilities. But new and emerging technologies are steadily changing this librarian/faculty paradigm.

Beginning with the implementation of on-line catalogs and remote access, continuing with CD-ROM databases, and more recently with access to networked electronic resources, libraries are becoming associated with technology and change. The only thing more remarkable than this change in user perception is the speed with which it is happening. Technology is rapidly changing the shape of scholarly communication and the library. These are changes that faculty cannot ignore; they can no longer depend solely on the skills they learned as fledgling researchers or on their familiarity with the narrower range of traditional library resources that have served their specialized interests. First in the sciences, next in the social sciences, and now in the humanities, the rapid changes in scholarly communication have raised interest and anxiety. In this way, new electronic tools have been a great motivator in opening up communication between librarians and the teaching faculty. Teachers and their students alike recognize the need to acquire new skills to succeed in the new information environment. Library administrators, too, now realize that for new technologies to be successful in meeting the faculty's and other library users' needs, instructional support must follow financial support and implementation of technology. In this way, new information technology is a force that breaks down the barriers between faculty and librarians and helps us gain recognition and status within the educational community. This can be an ally in creating a climate of collaboration for achieving broader educational goals.

Obviously, technology does not provide the reason or rationale for BI. Certainly, examples of BI successes and the articulation of BI principles predate the electronic revolution in libraries. The nationally recognized BI program at Earlham College (Farber 1993: 1–25) is just one, and possibly the best, example of such early successes. However, technology lends an energy and an urgency to BI, providing motivation on the part of students, faculty, and library administrators to acknowledge the educational mission of the library.

The debate over whether or not librarians should be full partners in the educational process is heard less often now. The debate has shifted from whether or not to teach to what to teach.

WHAT WE TEACH

Deciding "what" to teach was and perhaps still is the first challenge of BI. New information technologies have focused attention on this central issue of BI, and have played an important role in shifting the focus of BI from the library and library sources to information users and their needs (King and Baker 1987: 85–107).

Combined with the forces of changing demographics, technology has helped to subdivide and to splinter our perceptions of traditional academic library user groups. Where we once saw only undergraduates, graduate students, and faculty, we now notice new groups defined by skills, knowledge, and preparedness in using computers and new technology. Emerging information technologies have not caused but have brought into focus the diversity of our user groups and have compelled librarians to consider their unique needs in the delivery of library instruction. With mounting research on the barriers reentry, international, and other user populations face in achieving academic success, BI librarians have turned a spotlight on the importance of the library's role in meeting the unique needs of these groups and on the challenge and promise new information technologies provide (Wilson 1992: 20–53). In the past decade, the variety of library instructional efforts targeting adult, reentry, international, and economically disadvantaged students have had as their objective the desire to identify and then to overcome the lack of basic computer skills and in many cases the specter of library and computer anxiety within these groups.

We cannot make assumptions about an individual's familiarity with technology based on age, gender, academic status, or culture, but we now know that these differences and their combinations can impact educational outcomes when it comes to providing BI. Technology has sensitized us to potential differences in skill level and learning style among various user groups, as well as to the confusion constant and rapid technological change has caused for library users who have less than frequent contact with libraries and the changing electronic environment. We can easily tell how long it has been since a faculty member has been in the library by his or her bewilderment that a favorite print source is now provided through a different search engine and requires unfamiliar search commands and protocols. When doing general orientations to the library, it is now less appropriate to know a group's academic status than to know who among them are familiar with on-line catalogs and CD-ROM databases or have a PC and modem and have used networked resources.

What we teach should always be based on user needs. Do we teach technology? Yes, we must. Do we teach use of specific sources? Yes, we must. Do we teach process? Yes. Context? Yes. We should and must use everything we have learned from library and education research and its reported application to computers and BI. But we must remember that new technologies are not the focus of our instructional efforts; they are merely instruments for achieving larger instructional goals (Shill 1987: 433–453). Technology also requires us to resist the temptation to simplify the underlying or conceptual complexities inherent in increasingly user friendly systems. Likewise, we must avoid the temptation to make complex what is simple and intuitive. In an electronic environment, the practice of BI is often a delicate balancing act of deciding what to include and what to leave out. Users must learn how to exploit databases and search software as smart consumers, to expect and look for features such as on-line thesauri, the availability of cross-references, lateral and expanded search capabilities, truncation, field searching, or the strengths and weaknesses of free-term searching in a given database. However, it is not as important that students remember the details of searching a particular database or CD-ROM product as it is that they develop the longer-term skills of being able to identify the scope of a database; the appropriateness of content for their discipline, field, and topic; and to develop information skills around sound research principles, methodologies, and concepts.

New technologies will continue to present difficult teaching choices and to challenge our teaching methods. Often librarians teach to students (or faculty) as if they were teaching information science; helping users become better and more self-reliant information users does not mean making them into information specialists. If what we have to teach has value and content, we must allow students to build on their knowledge and skills through experience, as they would in mastering any other area of knowledge. Computers, with their rapid response to our keystrokes, may be great research aids, but they can send a wrong message to library users: that library research *is* keyboarding, and that it is quick, clean, and moves in a straight line from the InfoTrac terminal to the term paper. Sometimes, computing speed and the urgency of a blinking cursor can spill over into our own teaching styles. If we acknowledge that learning information technology skills is a process and not a 50-minute instructional cloudburst, we must resist trying to pour what we know into these students. More often than not they will capsize under the deluge. The pressures of technological change on BI efforts present the best case for course-integrated library instruction and the creation of an environment where librarians have contact with classes over time, and information skills are learned incrementally.

Networking and integration of CD-ROMs into OPAC interfaces and providing electronic gateways to Internet sources through Gophers, WAIS, and the World-Wide Web may have strong appeal to some librarians and sophisticated researchers, but will probably glaze over the eyes and boggle the minds of most library users. It is easy to forget that the simple division of libraries into undergraduate, graduate, and specialized subject collections is the first level of decision making to become blurred in electronic environments. In a virtual library environment, there is nothing to take the place of that simple organizational principle that organizes information by a users' ability to understand and digest it, not merely an ability to access it. It is not uncommon to see students in social sciences and humanities branch libraries wandering in electronic confusion through science-based sources that are not appropriate for their information needs, but which they have stumbled into because their databases are currently available through a CD-ROM LAN. They have made their way to the proper library building, but have taken an undesired and unknowing "virtual library" detour. If the student is in sight of the reference desk, it becomes an easily resolved reference issue. If the student is elsewhere, it is a BI issue with no easy solution.

The appropriate level of information needed by a user is just not apparent or addressed through an interface that organizes all information by format or subject content; matching information to a user's need has been the traditional role of BI and the reference interview. Intelligent, interactive interfaces may provide future assistance in this area, but for now, remote invisible users are at a distinct disadvantage in this regard. Invisible users are those who are not in sight of the reference desk. As library walls become increasingly translucent through the powerful combination of computers and telecommunications, it makes little difference whether we use the metaphor of invisible users or virtual libraries to frame the BI dilemma of providing direction and instructional opportunities to users made remote by technology.

Improvements in interface design have lagged far behind improvements in search engines or improvements in electronic access to and transfer of information. Will computer screen icons and "windowed" environments provide the conceptual frameworks for successful and efficient information seeking behaviors? This is a valid question with implications for BI. The appeal and wholesale success of the current generation of graphic user interfaces might suggest that they do. However, a case should be made that current icon-based interfaces reflect an intermediate phase in interface design, because they are not really intuitive and they force people to learn yet another computer language (O'Conner 1994: H2). Without a common icon grammar, will users have to learn the local icon dialect of each virtual library boundary they cross, or will some future generation of user interfaces solve the icon conundrum? Some instructional needs are and will continue to be driven by interface design.

If new technologies have given us new skills to teach, they have also made clear how fleeting the useful shelf life of many of these skills might be. In the search for a more meaningful and long-lived brand of BI, the Bibliographic Instruction Section of ACRL revised it's *Model Statement of Objectives for Academic Bibliographic Instruction* in 1987 to acknowledge that "the role of BI is not only to provide students with the specific skills necessary to complete assignments, but to prepare individuals to make effective life-long use of information. . . . By describing processes rather than tools, it is hoped that the Statement will remain effective long after the present new technology becomes old" (ACRL/BIS Task Force on Model Statement of Objectives 1987: 256–261). With the approval of these objectives in 1988 by the ALA Standards Committee, BI picked up the banner of information literacy and life-long learning, and launched an ongoing debate over the meaning, achievability, and appropriateness of such lofty goals for BI. When we talk about the impact of technology on what we teach, we can literally say that technology helped rewrite the objectives of BI, and launched the information skills versus information literacy debate. In an environment that is changing so rapidly and dynamically, BI librarians will continue to struggle with the question and the decision of "what to teach." The answers will change with new and emerging technologies, and it is not possible to predict what impact emerging technologies such as artificial intelligence, hypertext, voice recognition, or virtual reality will have on the BI objectives of information literacy or life-long learning. But it is likely that future technologies will require us to articulate the methods as well as we have articulated the vision of becoming an information literate society.

However, it is clear that information technologies present unique opportunities and challenges for BI. Hypertext linkages, search strategies incorporating a mix of natural language and controlled vocabularies, and the ability to search across disciplines and databases in single search sessions are much more than technological advancements in the management of information; they represent the first generation of technologies that compliment rather than prescribe the way we think. The language of information technology ("exploration," "navigation," "free-text searching") intuitively reflects these expanded learning opportunities. These new information technologies are not really library technologies; they are communication technologies, and through them we will learn new ways to communicate and new ways to teach.

THE WAY WE TEACH

If you are lucky enough to have access to a "wired" classroom, equipped with computers able to access your on-line catalog, CD-ROMs, and the Internet, along with an adequate computer projection system, you've got the basic components for using technology to teach. Other electronic capabilities might include additional stand-alone workstations, the ability to use and project both high-end DOS and Macintosh platforms, and video capability for use of videotape and live video projection. Nobody said technology for teaching came cheap. If this classroom is located in your library, so much the better, because you can combine your presentations conveniently with the use of relevant print sources. But location is not a requirement; accessibility for students, faculty, and librarians is. The ability to use technology to teach technology is one of the obvious positive impacts new technologies have had on BI. Technology has turned the library orientation into a library demonstration. And demonstrations are clearly effective formats for providing information skills training. It is the feedback, the interactivity of computers, that make them such wonderful teaching and learning tools. In a classroom setting, a computer projection system can make a classroom into an information learning laboratory where students can explore, experiment, and interact with computers and with each other. We must, of course, give them a chance to do just that. To use a wired classroom strictly for lecture format demonstrations is to deny the power of learning by doing. Giving over the keyboard is not giving up control. As this technology becomes increasingly portable, reliable, and affordable, and as more campus classrooms and dormitories become wired for access to remote information resources, instruction, too, becomes more portable. This portability has the potential to bring at least some of our invisible users into view.

When we talk about technology's impact on the way we teach, we have to include some discussion of presentation software, authoring software, and the largely unrealized potential of CAI (computer-assisted instruction) for BI. Presentation software gives us the capability to produce professional looking computerized slide presentations for computer projection or for output to 35-mm slides. The computerized slide presentations can be used as you would use transparencies for presentations or lectures. In addition to creating greater impact through color and graphics, some presentation software programs even allow for the incorporation of digitized motion video and sound. Although these programs are marketed for non-expert designers and have features such as ready-made graphic and text templates, fully exploiting the power and advanced features of such software and creating original programs "from scratch" with these systems will take time, practice, and, of course, the obvious additional hardware and software support necessary to create, capture, and customize graphics, video, and sound for incorporation into multimedia programs. Putting it all together effectively requires expertise in instructional and graphic design, or at least access to this expertise. Access to design expertise is even more important when using authoring software to create interactive instructional programs.

With the introduction of HyperCard by Apple Computers in 1987, there was hope that this new information tool would place the power of creating computer-assisted library instructional programs in the hands of the masses, or at least in the hands of the average BI librarian. For the first time, one didn't have to be a programmer type to create professional looking instructional software. There have certainly been some exciting experiments with and examples of HyperCard based instructional materials developed by librarians in-house as well as through commercial ventures such as *Research Assistant* (Bevilacqua 1993: 77–87). Educational applications of HyperCard are tracked and shared through Listserves, newsletters such as *ALUG* (Apple Library Users Group), library literature, and HISC (Hypermedia and Instructional Software Clearinghouse), a clearinghouse for educational HyperCard stacks.

However, HyperCard and authoring software relatives, such as SuperCard and Toolbook (for the DOS world), only highlight the need for BI librarians to collaborate with instructional designers, media specialists, and even those programmer types this very category of software hoped to bypass. Anyone who has authored in these programs would be less than truthful not to confess that these are complex, sophisticated design tools. They are wonderful multimedia construction kits, and the often used metaphor referring to them as electronic erector sets is quite appropriate:

"some assembly is required." At Arizona State University, we are fortunate to have access to both design and programming expertise through our own Department of Media Systems and through access to the resources of the University's Consortium for Instructional Innovation, which is operated under the University's Information Technology Unit to provide support for instructional software development. In-house, our library's Instructional Services Department has a full-time graphic artist. Not all BI programs enjoy this level of support; but whatever the level of support available, continued growth of the categories of software referred to as desktop publishing, desktop video, presentation software, and authoring software will continue to demand more time, more attention, more human resources, and more collaboration with others if the promise these technologies hold is to become fully realized.

The power and the potential of the computer to teach goes beyond the concept of using technology to teach technology. It touches on some of the most basic anxieties and insecurities we have about the importance, the uniqueness, and the effectiveness of our more traditional teaching methods.

CONCLUSION: WHY WE TEACH

This chapter has attempted to communicate the notion of how technology has impacted and transformed BI; from challenging us to reconsider what we teach to providing us opportunities for new ways to teach. But technology has also impacted "Why" we teach. A quick look backward will help explain.

When mediated, fee-based computer searching through database providers such as DIALOG and BRS was cutting-edge for libraries, librarians who gained expertise in selecting databases, conceptualizing search strategies, studying descriptors, balancing retrieval with precision, and manipulating search sets with Boolean commands felt newly empowered. Having mastered and then marketed these skills, it is not surprising that librarians would approach the emerging end-user environment of OPACs and CD-ROMs with trepidation and an untested mythology of how the general population of information seekers might learn end-user research skills.

At my own institution, when we introduced the first on-line catalog, I helped develop a 100-plus page users' manual to accompany the catalog. The manual was replete with detailed screen prints documenting any and all possible scenarios that users might encounter. This loose-leafed behemoth was conspicuously placed between each pair of on-line catalog terminals. Additionally, I wrote a special issue of our library's newsletter to faculty, explaining in detail the form and function of our new catalog, complete with an explanation of Boolean searching and a printed list of search commands. These, along with printed "tip" sheets, stacks of instructional bookmarks with more search commands, and a forest of instructional signage comprised the paper blizzard that introduced our new paperless catalog.

Of course, we now know that most library computer users would rather write a 20-page term paper than read a users' manual. But there is also another lesson here: to let go of the temptation to overmediate between technology and the user. Whether that mediation is a 100-plus page instruction manual or an overloaded eye-glazing lecture, when it comes to teaching tool-specific computer skills or critical thinking and information literacy skills, it is best to be a coach and a guide and then, as Lee Iacocca says in a popular commercial, to "get out of the way." The very term end-user is transitional, recalling the coexisting image of the librarian as a mediator between technology and the user. As long as we continue to think of those who interact directly with computerized information sources as end-users, we will remain in the shadow that the concept of mediation casts. We should understand that if the perceived remedial role instruction librarians play in the educational process has injured or threatened our self-image, it is a role we can change.

Short-term BI goals of teaching database-, network-, or tool-specific skills may very well soon be accomplished better or made less critical by computers through improved database and system design. This has already happened to a great extent as our individual experience, observation, and intuition of how users learn new technologies in our own libraries might confirm. Whether this will diminish the future role of librarians who currently provide user instruction or whether it will present opportunities for an expanded role under the banner of information literacy, as some current BI leaders believe, will remain for the future to reveal.

Information literacy has already been the focus of ALA committees (e.g., the ALA Presidential Committee on Information Literacy), the subject of books (e.g., Breivik and Gee 1989), the theme of conferences (e.g., the Seventeenth National LOEX Library Instruction Conference), and has provided the material for many, many journal articles and talks. Patricia Breivik, who chaired the ALA Presidential Committee on Information Literacy has said, "To be information literate, a person must be able to recognize when information is needed and have the ability to locate, evaluate, and use effectively the needed information" (Breivik 1989: 1–6). Paraphrasing from the report issued by that committee (American Library Association 1989), Breivik states that information literacy is "essential to the quality of individuals' lives, to business, and to our democratic way of life" (1989: 1–6). That's a tall order to fill, and not all BI practitioners are convinced that this objective is reasonable or achievable. Some might suggest that librarians are "overreaching" their responsibilities and their qualifications in claiming this ground as their own (Feinberg 1989: 83–85) and feel slighted by objectives that seem to devalue "the things we do best, such as teaching students library mechanics" (Feinberg and King 1988: 24–28). The information literacy debate and new and emerging information technologies are BI's two class troublemakers, and they always sit together; they upset our routines and challenge us to either change or to cope. Whether one believes that information literacy is an educational revolution, a mid-course correction, or the latest reworked educational slogan, the march of technology will demand that we articulate a new reason to teach that builds on and then moves beyond our current short-term, short-retention, technology-skill-based teaching objectives.

In conclusion, if one wanted a metaphor to compare the pre-electronic information environment with our current environment (and librarians love metaphors) one might say the pre-electronic library view of the information world was that of a mapped globe with each country a different color, and dense with small print naming countries, oceans, cities, and mountain ranges. Our current electronic library world view then would be (should be) the view from space, national boundaries and familiar land-marks blurred or invisible, our comfortable sense of place supplanted by a new sense of wonder and discovery, and perhaps an inkling of the interconnectedness of systems, people, and ideas. Technology has afforded us this new perspective, but technology does not humanize the image, does not make it meaningful, important, and useful to us as human beings. That is what teaching and education is about. And if BI is to be viable in the new electronic information age, this too, will have to be what BI is about. That is "why" we teach.

REFERENCES

American Library Association, Presidential Committee on Information Literacy. 1989. *Final Report.* Chicago: The Committee, ACRL/BIS Task Force on Model Statement of Objectives. 1987.

"Model Statement of Objectives for Academic Bibliographic Instruction: Draft Revision." *College and Research Libraries News* 48(5): 256–261.

Bevilacqua, Ann. 1993. "Research Assistant." In *Bibliographic Instruction in Practice: A Tribute to the Legacy of Evan Ira Farber.* Based on the 5th Earlham College-Eckerd College Bibliographic Instruction Conference, February 5–7, 1992. Ann Arbor: Pierian Press.

Breivik, Patricia Senn. 1989. "Information Literacy: Revolution in Education." In *Coping with Information Illiteracy: Bibliographic Instruction for the Information Age*. Betsy Baker and Mary Ellen Litzinger, ed. Papers presented at the Seventeenth National LOEX Library Instruction Conference held in Ann Arbor Michigan, May 4 and 5, 1989. Ann Arbor: Pierian Press.

Breivik, Patricia Senn, and E. Gordon Gee. 1989. *Information Literacy: Revolution in the Library*. New York: Macmillan.

Farber, Evan. 1993. "Bibliographic Instruction at Earlham College." In *Bibliographic Instruction in Practice: A Tribute to the Legacy of Evan Ira Farber*. Based on the 5th Earlham College-Eckerd College Bibliographic Instruction Conference, February 5–7, 1992. Ann Arbor: Pierian Press.

Feinberg, Richard. 1989. "Shorting-Out on Long Term Goals: A Different Perspective on Bibliographic Instruction and Information Literacy." In *Coping with Information Illiteracy: Bibliographic Instruction for the Information Age*. Betsy Baker and Mary Ellen Litzinger, eds. Papers presented at the Seventeenth National LOEX Library Instruction Conference held in Ann Arbor Michigan, May 4 and 5, 1989. Ann Arbor: Pierian Press.

Feinberg, Richard, and Christine King. 1988. "Short Term Library Skills Competencies: Arguing for the Achievable." *College & Research Libraries* 49(1): 24–28.

King, David, and Betsy Baker. 1987. "Human Aspects of Library Technology: Implications for Academic Library User Education." In *Bibliographic Instruction: The Second Generation*. Constance A. Mellon, ed. Littleton, CO: Libraries Unlimited, Inc.

O'Conner, Roy. 1994. "Macintosh Revolution Battling New Roadblocks." January 30, *Arizona Republic* H: 2.

Shill, Harold B. 1987. "Bibliographic Instruction: Planning for the Electronic Information Environment." *College & Research Libraries* 48(5): 433–453.

Wilson, Lizabeth A. 1992. "Changing Users: Bibliographic Instruction for Whom." In *The Evolving Educational Mission of the Library*. Betsy Baker and Mary Ellen Litzinger, eds. Chicago: Bibliographic Instruction Section, Association of College & Research Libraries, A Division of the American Library Association.

4 The Impact of Emerging Technologies on Library Clientele

John C. Tyson

The National Information Infrastructure (NII) and the National Research and Education Network (NREN) initiatives place high hopes on emerging information technologies to improve the delivery of information services to the average library client. Even though these emerging technologies will play an important role in providing access to end-users, can we be certain that the average citizen will have the requisite skills and knowledge to navigate the NREN to obtain the information he or she seeks? Currently, many practicing librarians do not have the necessary training and support to provide library clients with access to electronic information services; therefore, it is not realistic to presuppose that the average student, business person, or scholar would have these special skills. A necessary first step would be to ensure that all information specialists working in libraries receive training to serve as intermediaries in connecting library clients to local, statewide, and global electronic networks and in guiding users to appropriate information resources via these networks. Once the library workforce is trained, it will be incumbent on the library profession to assist in educating and training the citizenry at large, since in many instances library clients will be able to obtain information services without traveling to a particular library location.

An important question for consideration is whether information technology will make it easier for all library clientele—rural and urban, young and old, affluent and impoverished—to obtain basic information services or, will these emerging technologies further widen the gap between the information "haves" and "have nots" and simply increase the advantages that educated, technically proficient citizens have over those less so? Will these emerging technologies simplify the provision of information services or will they add yet another layer of complexity to the already confusing manner in which the networks organize information services?

This chapter focuses on the impact of these emerging technologies on average library clients who, for the most part, will be accessing information from their homes, offices, and laboratories without physically traveling to a library and without the on-site assistance of an information professional.

It is clear that the NII will be able to provide equitable access to technologically proficient users; however, what is not clear is who will be responsible for training the millions of citizens who are not computer or information literate, particularly adults who are beyond the years of formal schooling. There are many things that libraries could and should do over the next decade. The suggestions offered in this chapter represent a "best effort" at selecting those areas in which libraries need to focus their resources to have the most positive effect on bridging the gap between access and delivery.

During the next decade, it is imperative that academic, public, school, institutional, and corporate libraries enthusiastically join the national education reform movement to address this need through the development of formal learning opportunities designed to impart knowledge of information literacy skills that focus specifically on three functional areas. Library clients will require considerable assistance and training in (1) understanding how information is structured, (2) obtaining technical skills needed to exploit fully the emerging information technologies, and (3) acquiring the ability to critically evaluate the information once found. Knowledgeable librarians will play a key role in assisting end-users in locating information and learning these critical new skills. Specific learning opportunities will need to be integrated into the formal educational curriculum starting with kindergarten through twelfth grade (K–12) to be built on throughout life. Libraries will have the potential to enrich the personal and professional lives of all citizens who possess these critical competencies.

Without question, emerging information technologies will have a tremendous impact on the quality of life in the twenty-first century. Practically every aspect of life will revolve around the creation and exchange of information. To ensure equitable participation in society, all citizens, regardless of location or socioeconomic status, will require access to a broader set of telecommunications services, among them a basic package of library and public information services.

For example, imagine the following scenario: The year is 1999. A family of four has just moved into their new home, which is wired with fiber-optic cable providing them access to a variety of digitized services. Through a kitchen workstation, the parents send a registered message via the local "freenet" to their school board representative. They also check the bulletin board for the next school board meeting agenda and county election date. Noticing a citizen survey request, via the same bulletin board, they record their opinions on the county's information services via an electronic bulletin board.

Also, due to the mother's current jury duty assignment, she reviews the court docket and her attendance requirements. Meanwhile, their daughter, a high school student, has just completed her homework on an interactive workbook-information system using another workstation in the den. She also participates in her evening distance learning class in French. She settles in front of her television with the portable phone for verbal and written interactions with her French instructor located in Paris, France. She passes the exam for that evening's class.

The son, a college student, is at the local public library where he has come to retrieve books that he requested from the workstation at home. While in the library, he does one-stop shopping for information services through a multimedia kiosk and his "smart card." The menu not only provides access to the NREN, but also to job openings by geographic area. He is also able to register to vote and obtain a copy of his birth certificate. His smart card serves as his library card, social security card, driver's license, medical services card, hunting and fishing license, and electronic benefits card. Local, state, and federal government agencies using a common information infrastructure will make this scenario a reality for most citizens during the next decade.

COMPUTER LITERACY AND INFORMATION LITERACY

The term "literacy" is generally defined as the ability to read and write. In the past, during the Agricultural and Industrial ages, basic educational literacy was considered adequate to function in society, to achieve one's goals, and to develop one's knowledge and potential. Today, and even more so in the future, these skills alone will be considered inadequate to function fully in the Information Age. Two additional competencies will be needed to function successfully and competitively in our global economy, that is, computer literacy and information literacy. Simply put, citizens who possess these two higher levels of skills will be able to function independently. End-users without these critical skills will be dependent on others to access information needed to make decisions in their daily lives. The ability to access electronic databases independently, to extract multiple features of information in lengthy and sometimes complex displays, and to compare, contrast, and evaluate that information from a workstation in one's home, office, or local library will be considered basic skills. Citizens who do not possess these critical skills are far more likely to be unemployed and in poverty and are far less likely to be in professional, managerial, or technical positions.

Within the last decade, our libraries have grown more technologically advanced as evidenced by the growing numbers of libraries that have access to the Internet. Many argue that this is eloquent testimony to support greater funding for training staff and patrons in the new technologies. As the Internet evolves into the more comprehensive NREN, which is envisioned to become an interconnection of the nation's educational infrastructure, this argument becomes more compelling. In this system, elementary schools, high schools, colleges, and universities will be linked with research centers and laboratories so that all may share access to libraries, databases, and diverse scientific instruments such as supercomputers, telescopes, and particle accelerators. The ability to read, write, and calculate are prerequisites to learning computer and information literacy skills. According to the latest survey results many adults do not demonstrate these proficiencies even at the most basic level—eighth grade reading, writing, and arithmetic.

The National Adult Literacy Survey, conducted by Educational Testing Services for the U.S. Department of Education, is the largest, most comprehensive study ever conducted of the literacy skills of America's adults. During the first eight months of 1992, more than 26,000 individuals across the nation gave more than an hour of their time to participate in the survey, performing a series of applied literacy tasks and answering a set of background questions on their education, labor force experiences, reading practices, demographic characteristics, and other topics. The results offered a detailed portrait of the educational literacy skills of America's adults.

According to Irwin Kirsch, executive director of Educational Testing Service, the needs are great. Nearly half of the adults nationwide—or nearly 100 million persons aged 16 or older—performed in the two lowest levels of literacy defined. These individuals appear to be at risk in a society in which literacy is a key to opportunity. According to the survey, literacy is inextricably linked with employment and economic status.

THE LIBRARY'S ROLE IN CREATING AN
INFORMATION LITERATE SOCIETY

Libraries have played a key role in America's cultural and economic development for almost 400 years. Every library in America will have a role to play in ensuring that library clientele who need or wish to improve their information literacy skills have the opportunity to do so. It is also important that library patrons themselves come to realize the value of computer and information literacy in their lives and to recognize the advantages associated with having these critical skills.

Libraries must continue to play a proactive role in ensuring equitable access and use of information systems regardless of the library client's social and economic status. A key leadership role should focus on promoting the acquisition and use of information technology in schools, libraries, and workplaces to create a computer-literate society. At the same time, we must avoid creating disparity between the information rich and the information poor. Traditionally, libraries have been known for providing collective access to monographs and serials that no individual could hope to afford. Today, library materials are more expensive than ever. The average reference book costs more than many families would be able to pay.

Librarians must play a leadership role in developing the community infrastructure of libraries, schools, community centers, churches, and other local agencies to facilitate training, education, and implementation of formal information literacy programs. Efforts to teach library clientele to become familiar with information technology will not be complete unless we acknowledge the fact that there are many groups that may need special attention. The role of libraries will be to work with the telecommunications industry to provide all consumers and all businesses with reasonably priced access, not only to electronic databases, but to the full complement of advanced video and data services that will come. Information in all its formats must be available to the people. This access will give new stimulus to the economy through the information intensive businesses that experts predict will account for much of our nation's future growth and job creation. It is projected that in the twenty-first century, most homes and offices will be connected to a new, high-capacity telecommunications infrastructure.

Among the groups that may need special attention are regular users of the library; adult students, international students, students with disabilities, and members of minority groups. In fact, it is projected that by the year 2000, almost one third of the population of the United States will be composed of members of the four predominant minority groups, which are projected to grow at a rate faster than the population as a whole. Whereas these special library clientele will constitute a major segment of the workforce and will contribute substantially to the economic well-being of the nation, they must have the knowledge and skills to use the new information technologies in the workplace as well as in their homes. In regards to special needs, librarians should be cognizant of statistics that support the fact that library users from minority groups are more likely to have completed fewer years of school in this country than white individuals. Also, many Asian/Pacific Islanders and Hispanic adults are born in other countries and speak English as a second language. Educating library clientele to become competent in accessing the NREN and understanding various types of electronic services will become an important facet of library instruction. Libraries will be challenged to help the growing number of library patrons with special needs develop expertise in library use.

THE NEED FOR CURRICULUM REFORM

The U.S. National Commission on Libraries and Information Science has concluded that a philosophical commitment must be made to information literacy as a guiding principle of learning by public policy makers and school superintendents, principals, teachers, library media specialists, and educational researchers. Our nation's ability to compete will be strengthened by investing in computer and information literacy skills for our children. The ability to access and effectively use information throughout one's life will be an essential ability of a literate person in the twenty-first century. Further, the ability to locate, to understand, to evaluate, and to use information correlates closely with a student's ability to succeed in school, in college, and in the workplace.

America's workplace is changing. Training for one job that will last a lifetime is no longer a viable approach to career education since people change jobs many times. The future workforce will need more highly developed skills. By the year 2000, the number of unskilled jobs will decline from 9 percent of all jobs today to just 4 percent, while the number of jobs requiring substantial skills will double to 41 percent of the job market. In 1991, the U.S. Department of Labor concluded that those who will find employment in the future should have the following attributes: basic skills such as reading, writing, mathematics, speaking and listening; thinking skills such as creativity, decision making, reasoning, and problem solving; and personal qualities such as individual responsibility, self-management, and integrity.

In addition to these attributes, the impact of emerging information technology will require another layer of skills. If meaningful curriculum reform is to take place, libraries will need to join forces with schools, businesses, and community organizations to sponsor projects that address these skills and competencies. A national training model for information literacy skills will need to serve both library clientele and providers of information. Superintendents and principals will need to create a vision about information literacy that will redefine, redesign, and reaffirm the school library media program in relation to the goal of having every student graduate from high school with at least basic information literacy skills. Just as our nation provides entitlement to all citizens for basic public education, the nation must make a commitment to provide information literacy training for persons of all ages, and particularly through the level of high school graduation. Adults who have not attained basic computer and information literacy skills will need to be educated. The goal is to have a literate workplace; however, this can be attained only if an adequate foundation program is available for citizens and especially students in all schools, no matter what their location or circumstances. Library educators must invest time in curriculum design and encourage collaboration among librarians and teachers in the various disciplines and encourage teamwork and integrated curricula.

CUSTOMER SERVICE: THE KEY TO SUCCESSFULLY MARKETING LIBRARY SERVICES TO CLIENTELE

With shrinking budgets these are difficult, challenging times for libraries. The developing pressures of the twenty-first century will require libraries to move in directions that depart from cherished tradition. A major concern centers around the inability of libraries to provide an adequate number of qualified staff, appropriate information technologies, collections, support programs, and services that meet the needs of its primary clientele. Budget reductions make it more difficult each year. However, these basic services are essential if we are to remain effective in addressing the information needs of library clientele in the future.

Who will the major competitions for libraries be in the year 2000? The large and growing private information industry functions in part by taking information traditionally provided free by libraries, adding value to it, and reselling it to the public. There are thousands of private sector information companies who claim they can provide access to information more cost effectively than libraries. Libraries throughout the nation are reducing services because of lost budget battles with fire departments, police departments, and other essential services. What can libraries do to guarantee their survival in the next century, even if it is proven that the private sector can provide some traditional library services for less money? Libraries must focus their energies and resources on the diverse needs of its local clientele. Furthermore, they must empower their constituency through user-friendly access to the specific information and services they need. The unique niche for libraries in the future will depend on their ability to convince public policy makers that they have a meaningful role to play in the economic revitalization of local communities through the provision of information.

Libraries that base their service philosophy on providing all citizens with equitable access regardless of their educational levels, special needs, economic status, and ethnicities will be in a good position to compete with the private sector. Libraries may wish to gather data through community needs assessments to examine local library clientele attitudes about technology. A needs assessment can help determine if the majority of library users are "technocrats," "technophobes," or someone in between. Many adults have yet to become computer literate. Academic librarians are reporting that, contrary to popular belief, many of today's college students will suffer from "technostress." For these reasons, libraries must market themselves as user-friendly. Librarians will need to go into the communities and make citizens aware of their willingness to teach information literacy skills. Once patrons are in the library, first-class customer service enables the organization to maintain a supportive and loyal customer base.

Libraries cannot assume automatic funding in the future because of past successes. They must be perceived by citizens as being effective and efficient. This means that standards for customer service are identified in terms of client satisfaction, increased public awareness, and fulfillment of a client's information need. Library staff will need techniques for dealing with people on the telephone, for helping people in face-to-face communications, as well as working with people who are angry, hostile, or upset. Customer service means simply being nice to people in such a way that they remember you, your library, and value the personal satisfaction they got because of working with you. The difference between customer service and satisfaction may be the difference between voter loyalty and voter rejection when bond issues and other budgetary matters come before the citizenry for approval. Satisfied library clients will tell three or four people their "satisfied-customer" stories but unhappy clients are likely to tell eight to ten. The ultimate goal for libraries is to have employees who focus their energy and talents on people-oriented tasks while the emerging technologies are used to do routine, competitive tasks.

Information technology can be used to improve efficiency; however, staff will determine library effectiveness. The benefits for becoming more customer oriented are many—increased efficiency, enhanced morale, expanded employee pride, and greatly increased customer satisfaction from establishing quality service as a serious organizational goal. During times of decreased resources, a renewed focus on the end-user provides a basis for redefining priorities, and provides an impetus for work units to cooperate more fully.

CONCLUSION

The American public will need to be provided basic computer and information literacy skills to ensure that the average citizen can take advantage of the emerging information technologies. Libraries, working in cooperation with education institutions, will have an important leadership role to play in creating educational opportunities to ensure that the provision of information is simplified and not made more difficult.

The various initiatives at the national, regional, state, and local levels to provide infrastructure are important. They provide vision and general direction, but do not offer the detailed policy guidance that will be needed to speed the transition toward equitable delivery of information for library clients.

Without question, the Information Age will offer unprecedented opportunities for academic, public, school, institutional, and corporate libraries to work together, share collections, and use common technology systems to deliver information through single-access points.

This chapter has identified several components essential to delivering quality information services for library clientele in the twenty-first century. Citizens will depend on libraries to provide useful, accurate, and timely information more than ever. Information is the new currency of the world, and libraries give citizens access to it. Libraries will enable all citizens to participate in an economy where information is the major commodity. Open access to public information held by library and government agencies is a cornerstone of our democratic system. Ironically, new technologies and growing fiscal pressures will create serious challenges that threaten the ability of library clientele to access information without intervention from an information specialist. Libraries will need to market themselves in terms of their contribution to the public good.

The most important issue relating to the impact of emerging technologies on library clientele is that of accessibility. In a knowledge-based society, information has value as a commodity. Those who are in a position to access it or purchase it will have the advantage over those who are not in that position. An important role for libraries in the future will be to serve as community access points where all citizens can receive access if the technology is not available in one's home or office. Historians remind us that during the last 200 years our nation's literacy skills have increased dramatically in response to new requirements and expanded opportunities for social and economic growth. Today, we are a better-educated and more-literate society than at any time in our history. However, to bridge the gap from where we are and where we will need to be as a literate society in the twenty-first century will require a significant leadership role from the nation's libraries.

REFERENCES

American Library Association Presidential Committee on Information Literacy Final Report. 1989. Chicago: American Library Association.

Anderson, Charles. 1990. "Impact of the New Technology on Patrons and Staff." *Wilson Library Bulletin* 64 (February): 69–70.

Behrens, Shirley J. 1992. "Librarians and Information Literacy." *Mousaion* 10: 81–88.

Bjorner, Susan N. 1991. "The Information Literacy Curriculum—A Working Model." *IATUL Quarterly* 5 (June): 150–160.

Breivik, Patricia S., and E. Gordon Gee. 1989. *Information Literacy: Revolution in the Library.* New York: Macmillan Publishing Company.

Carnevale, A. P., A. S. Gainer, A. S. Meltzer, and S. L. Holland. 1988. "Workplace Basics: The Skills Employees Want." *Training and Development Journal* (October): 20–30.

Carroll, J. B., and J. S. Chall, eds. 1975. *Toward a Literate Society: A Report from the National Academy of Education.* New York: McGraw-Hill.

Demo, William. 1986. *The Idea of Information Literacy in the Age of High-Tech.* Dryden, New York: Educational Resources Information Center.

Eisenberg, Michael B., and Kathleen L. Spitzer. 1991. *Annual Review of Information Science and Technology* 26: 243–285.

Grand Challenges: High Performance Computing and Communication. 1992. Washington, DC: U.S. Research and Development Program.

Information Literacy and Education for the 21st Century. 1989. Washington, DC: U.S. National Commission on Libraries and Information Science.

Information 2000: Library and Information Services for the 21st Century, Summary Report of the 1992 White House Conference on Library and Information Services. 1991. Washington, DC: NCLIS.

Kirsch, Irwin S., Ann Jungeblut, Lynn Jenkins, and Andrew Kolstad. *Adult Literacy in America.* 1993. Washington, DC: U.S. Department of Education, National Center for Education Statistics.

Martin, Susan K. 1989. "Library Management and Emerging Technology: The Immovable Force and the Irresistible Object." *Library Trends* 37 (Winter): 374–382.

McCrank, Lawrence S. 1992. "Academic Programs for Information Literacy: Theory and Structure." *RQ* 31 (Summer): 485–497.

Moran, Barbara B. 1984. *Academic Libraries: The Changing Knowledge Center of College and Universities.* Washington, DC: Association for the Study of Higher Education.

Naito, Marilyn. 1991. "An Information Literacy Curriculum: A Proposal." *College and Research Libraries News* 52 (May): 293–296.

Natke, Nora Jane. 1992. "Emerging Technologies in Resource Sharing and Document Delivery." *Journal of Youth Services in Libraries* 5 (Winter): 189–192.

Olsen, Jan K., and Bill Coons. 1989. *Information Literacy Issue Paper.* Chicago: American Library Association.

Plesser, Ronald L., and E. W. Cividanes. 1993. *Serving Citizens in the Information Age: Access Principles for State and Local Government Information.* Washington, DC: Information Industry Association.

Rader, Hannelore, and Bill Coons. 1989. *Information Literacy Background, Learning Goals and Objectives.* Chicago: American Library Association.

Report Brief. 1993. Washington, DC: U.S. Congress, Office of Technology Assessment. (November).

Roszak, Theodore. 1986. "Partners for Democracy: Public Libraries and Information Technology." *Wilson Library Bulletin* 60 (February): 14–17.

Strategic Plan for the Future of Library Services in Massachusetts. 1993. Boston: Massachusetts Board of Library Commissioners.

Sullivan, Laura A., and Nancy F. Campbell. 1991. "Strengthening the Foundation for Information Literacy in an Academic Library." *Reference Librarian* 33: 183–189.

Ward-Callaghan, Linda. 1987. "The Effect of Emerging Technologies on Children's Library Service." *Library Trends* 35 (Winter): 437–447.

5 People, Organizations, and Information Technology: Facing the Millennium

Delmus E. Williams

As librarianship approaches the end of the twentieth century, it is becoming increasingly clear that the profession has changed radically over the last twenty years and that the pace at which change is occurring is increasing. Although librarians are still being asked to bring users together with the resources required to meet their information needs, the environment in which they work is becoming ever more complex. The purpose of this chapter is to examine how this kind of continuous change will affect library organizations in general and public service programs in particular. It will also examine what those who are being asked to provide leadership for reference and other public service programs will have to do to cope with their new environment.

THE MANAGEMENT OF LIBRARY SERVICES

Libraries are very traditional organizations. They defined their mission in the quarter century before World War I and then developed a set of tools and structures reflecting the technologies and fashion of that time. Over the next 75 years, libraries have become much larger than library pioneers might have expected them to be, but the primary source of information available is still the book; the primary finding tools are still card catalogs and printed indexes; and the primary role of the librarian continues to be one in which he or she meets the needs of users within the context of the book stock of the library in which he or she works.

William G. Bowen (1992) recently described libraries as "the symbols of the continuity of learning" (p. xi), and this continuity has made them very predictable supports for a learned community that changes very slowly. This constancy is not unwelcomed. Libraries, as a class, have done what they do well, and they have accomplished the mission assigned to them while remaining comfortable and predictable places, both for those who work in them and for those who use them (Moran 1994).

That is not to discount the changes that began to occur in the way information was being distributed on campus and in the community in the late 1960s and early 1970s. By 1975, instructors on most college campuses had begun to use instructional media in the classroom, and computers were being introduced to manage tasks like accounting and payroll in all kinds of organizations. But more often than not, these technologies were either viewed as alien to the library and supported by separate organizations within the university or were administered much as print collections had always been managed and used as a "better" book or chalkboard to perform very specialized functions. The idea that media could be more than a supplement to traditional instructional methods was not taken seriously. People who used it as a major element in their courses were generally viewed as shirkers who did not want to prepare for class. The idea that someone who used media extensively might be innovative was less well accepted than was the image of the stereotypical football coach in the *Funky Winkerbean* comic strip who can only face a class if there is a film to show.

Library organizations have changed little since 1920. They have retained the bureaucratic structure they embraced at the turn of the century (Lynch 1978). Their use of administrative tiers has given library managers a secure way to control its operations and has also provided its staff and faculty an opportunity for professional growth. Libraries have become adept at integrating new ideas into their bureaucracies, as opposed to reforging their organizations to accommodate changes in their environment or in their programs. As a result, library organizations have evolved gradually, enabling those who work in them to survive and prosper with little understanding of how organizations work and a minimum of exposure to alternative models.

The slowness with which changes have taken place in library programs and the organizations that support these programs has allowed librarians to survive with little more than the skills learned in library school. This has been particularly useful in that many librarians have not been comfortable with the automation of library operations and have been reluctant to prepare themselves to cope with this change. The capacity of the bureaucracy to slow down change while its professional staff digested new ideas has helped the profession adapt to its new environment gradually without presenting too much of a threat to its workers and users.

The task of the library manager has changed little in that same last 75-year period. That person is still expected to find funding to purchase, catalog and store ever expanding book stocks and to recruit and train a workforce that could manipulate existing, paper-based technologies. In the same vein, library workers are still asked to serve the needs of clients who are either white and middle class or who address the library and resources as if they are.

But times have begun to change. OCLC's appearance in the mid-1960s convinced the library community that computers have a place in the library. After that, the dramatic increase in the capabilities of computers, the growing sophistication of computer software, and the equally dramatic reduction in computer costs have made online systems a staple in every library budget. The elimination of the card catalog and the introduction of other electronic tools have changed the way libraries look, and not everyone has approved of these changes. Nicolson Baker (1994) recently called the destruction of card catalogs a "paroxysm of shortsightedness and anti-intellectualism (in a class with the burning of the library at Alexandria)" (p. 64). But change has come nonetheless.

As libraries have begun to rely more heavily on technology, they have just now begun the process of adapting to this change. Barbara Moran (1994) noted that the adoption of new technology generally comes in three stages. In the first stage, the technology is used to do things that have been done before. In the second, it is applied to new areas. In the third, technology becomes a transformational agent that leads to fundamental change in organizations. To date, libraries have, for the most part, been operating in the first phase, using technology almost exclusively to do things that they have done before. The primary role assigned to computers thus far has been to produce more easily products that have long been used in libraries or to perform clerical tasks faster and more efficiently than was previously possible. OCLC's first function was to provide a better way to generate cards for a card catalog, and most early DIALOG databases were simply more accessible, complete, and current periodical indexes. And, until recently, automated catalogs were not radically different in concept from the card catalogs that they replaced.

It is true that fewer people now work behind the scenes and that a larger percentage of the library's resources are now available for public services as computers have made technical services more efficient (De Klerk and Euster 1989). It is also true that programs have been introduced to educate users on the expanding array of information services and resources that are available and that librarians have acquired new skills to help them interface with online data files and interpret these resources to a more diverse group of patrons. And, of course, the increasing cost of journals and books have made libraries more dependent on interlibrary cooperation and interlibrary lending. But most of the changes that have taken place so far have either been designed to absorb technical marvels without changing anything or applying new machinery to old problems. They have merely been designed to provide logical extensions of traditional library services.

THE NEW WORLD OF INFORMATION RESOURCES

The maturation of the microcomputer as a technology and the increasing sophistication of telecommunications are beginning to have a transformational effect on the information industry. At the same time, the cost of traditional services is moving beyond the reach of the library as the cost of journals and other printed materials rise precipitously. It is becoming increasingly obvious that it is no longer enough to introduce incremental changes in the way organizations transfer information. Libraries must soon move into Moran's second phase in the introduction of technology and perhaps beyond it. Robert C. Heterick (1993) and others have begun to talk about reengineering the classroom to deliver information more cost effectively, and libraries must follow suit if they are to meet the needs of those who use them.

The capacity of information technology to tailor information to the needs of the user is making the way librarians and others have approached information management obsolete. The amount of information available to libraries and the array of tools that must be used to access that information adds complexity to the way service is provided. In addition, the range of sophistication among users has changed the way libraries do business. The mission is changing from one that focused on collecting and servicing collections to one that focuses on delivering increasing amounts of information to users at a lower cost.

Technology has become the key to the library's success in meeting this challenge. Librarians are being stretched into new areas. On the one hand, information professionals are faced with a requirement to provide more user instruction relating to a wider array of technologies. On the other, their authority as masters of the information industry is being challenged as they are introduced regularly to patrons who can use the new tools available to them at least as well as they can. At the same time, the willingness of academic institutions to invest resources in these programs is declining.

Information technologies that do not rely on paper are not new to libraries. But, as noted earlier, microcomputers and fiber-optic communications are transforming the information industry more than those technologies that preceded them. Their impact on American life has been as revolutionary as was the introduction of the Model T at the turn of the century. The low-cost automobile democratized travel in the United States by affording the average person the capacity to see what life was like outside of his or her neighborhood. The microcomputer and advances in telecommunications have democratized access to information by making it possible for people to get answers to their questions from anywhere in the world. Users now have or will soon have at their fingertips all of the information being generated anywhere. The only limitations that they face relate to the equipment that they have available to them and their own capacity to find and use that information.

This kind of access to information has profound implications for the role of librarians as information brokers. Powerful, dependable, and inexpensive computers and fast, reliable telecommunications lines with bands wide enough to feed data, voice, and images through the same channels have commercial providers, university administrators, and librarians rethinking their service programs. Although it is not at all clear that paper is going to be superseded completely as electronic resources become available, the inflation rates associated with print materials are providing ample encouragement to libraries to make investments in alternative sources of information. Computers working with laser pictures over high quality telephone lines can provide print resources on demand at a price that is increasingly competitive with that of ongoing journal subscriptions. This trend is apparently here to stay and libraries are likely to continue their drift away from collecting toward programs designed to provide access to external resources.

The emergence of wide area networking (WAIS) and increases in the usage of a variety of information resources available through Internet, Prodigy, the proposed National Information Infrastructure, and a variety of other commercial services offers a challenge as the library sees its role as the primary source for information changing to accommodate alternative resources.

As more patrons approach the library and other information sources electronically rather than physically, the library must rethink its roles as an information provider and as an information broker. The library will undoubtedly see the mix of technologies with which it and its patrons must cope to expand further. First, the library must fit multimedia and imaging into its programs, and then it must explore other delivery devices as the information environment continues to develop. The challenge for the information professional working in public services will be to ensure that patrons who may or may not be located in a library facility can get to and can use effectively resources located in the library collections, housed in other libraries, or available through electronic networks.

They must also be prepared for a change in their clientele. Libraries have always had to deal with varied levels of sophistication in their users. But librarians have always been the experts who introduced patrons to systems, standards, and value sets that they understood better than anyone else. Increasingly, however, the Internet, CD-ROMs, and other electronic data files are moving away from this kind of universality as they produce resources with little regard for common conventions. Making the best use of the new resources is likely to require a joint effort that utilizes the skills and talents of both information providers and users of that information. Projects like the Information Arcade at the University of Iowa that integrate the efforts of the library, the computer center, and the academic faculty to provide the resources needed to support the teaching-learning process. This attempt to bring together the resources of the library, the computer center, and the teaching faculty in a facility that provides support for teaching innovation while encouraging self-sufficiency has much to offer as a model (Lowry 1994). Efforts like this that are designed to link traditional print resources with electronic ones to help transform the way teachers teach and students learn provide a model for future service programs. To succeed, they will require new linkages to ensure that teachers with imagination can be brought together with the resources that they need to support their efforts quickly and at the lowest possible cost to the institution.

LEGACIES WITHIN THE LIBRARY

As important as these changes are to the future of the library, it is critical that the library also take care of the business that it has built over the years. Librarians and others have long discussed the imminent demise of paper as the preferred mechanism for delivering information. But, to date, book stocks in libraries are still their most important information resource. This is not likely to change in the next few years. Paper has much to offer as a convenient, useful, and inexpensive technology, and many scholars continue to view it as their primary means of scholarly communication. Although economic factors and an information glut are encouraging a move away from print, it is unlikely that this movement will eliminate the need for library managers to stock and provide access to voluminous print collections for at least the next 25 years. Even if the information industry radically transforms the way journals and monographs are produced and used and those who counsel users can wean scholars away from books, the book stocks that are currently in libraries cannot be easily transformed into electronic formats for some time to come. As a result, the movement from a print collection to a virtual library will take some time to complete. So long as these print collections remain, libraries will be required to provide large storage facilities, finding tools that are designed to help the user navigate within those facilities, and stacks maintenance and circulation control systems designed to manage library inventories.

Existing library staffs have training and skills that both help and hinder their effectiveness in a changing world. Those who are now charged with providing leadership for the library community were trained in a different era. Library school graduates of the early 1970s came to the profession with a strong commitment to service and to user education, and they were taught to be better at developing and using complex text databases than anyone else.

These traits prepare them for the future, but others are less helpful. Many library workers were attracted to the field because of its conservatism. It was a safe haven in a changing world, and many were not prepared to cope with the electronic delivery systems that have emerged. Library managers were taught to use lengthy planning processes that emphasized frugality and limited risk, and their reliance on these models has limited the flexibility of the organizations that they lead to meet changing demands. Attempts to upgrade the skills of working librarians are succeeding slowly, but commitments to earlier mind sets remain. As Falduto, Blythe, and McClure (1994) noted, "it is faster and easier to install technology than to restructure our work and reculture our organizations" (p. 7). Libraries have staked their survival on keeping the tail-lights of those who are changing the information in sight rather than by trying to lead the movement, and this has allowed library professionals to make the changes at their own pace. But this is becoming an increasingly risky tactic.

THE CHALLENGE OF A NEW ERA

While libraries and those who lead them are entering a period in which technology is demonstrating its capacity to support services and products that were not possible without it, the information industry is moving quickly toward the third stage, a time when these services will transform both library organizations and those supporting other information services. To survive and prosper, libraries must develop an understanding of changes in the world of information and then provide a program that bridges the gap between what they are now and what they have always done and what they must be and do in the new century. It is not enough to speculate about what the future will bring in the way of new technologies or new organizational structures. Although that future is close at hand, it is not clear which of these technologies will win an audience, which will die, and what new resources will appear that have not yet entered the marketplace. Libraries must watch carefully for these developments, but the most difficult task facing them may be the requirement to build new service programs on the platform provided by existing organizations and existing personnel.

Libraries cannot afford to discard what they now have for something that may change overnight. The strengths of library organizations must be maintained as a foundation on which new programs can be built. Although change will come, many of the fundamental things libraries do will remain the same. But a successful transition will require libraries to keep their eye on the future, remain flexible, and take advantage of future opportunities. They must, in the view of William Bergquist (1993), develop a clear mission designed to serve as a "sea anchor"—that is, a mission designed to allow them to follow the tide while stabilizing them when the water becomes rough. They must constantly look at existing programs with an eye toward refining that mission, adapt existing programs to changing situations where possible, discard programs that cannot be supported or that have become obsolete, and build on a commitment to provide the best possible service to their constituencies. As Sheila Creth (1994) noted, librarians must resist the natural impulse to let the past define the future. They must be willing to rethink their assumptions and prepare to initiate the kind of fundamental changes that will eventually be required to transform their organizations.

As fiber-optics-based telecommunications systems develop to the point where they can deliver video, voice, and data over the same wires, more questions will arise. Organizations must decide who will administer and distribute various kinds of data, where the wires should run, what services will be required to ensure that the campus can use the full potential of this kind of system, and what skills will be needed to help people use them. It may be necessary to merge the campus library, computer center, and the media production and distribution facilities, or it may not. But it will be increasingly difficult to separate the functions now served by these organizations based on format or delivery mechanisms when all of the information they provide comes through the same channel. Service programs must be developed that look at information delivery as a single campus activity, and structures must be designed to support those services.

Planning for adequate information services must take into account this convergence in information technology and understand that segregation based on technical considerations may be increasingly difficult to justify. The Internet has already begun to blur the distinction between the kind of data that is supported by the computer center and the information resources of the library. The further development of more sophisticated journals and other tools delivered in electronic formats will make these lines even fuzzier as they unite the user, the author and the publisher into a single community using the same tools and sharing common interests and needs.

Internet, Bitnet, and commercial networks providing similar services are creating a situation in which anyone can author material and offer it to the world with little capital and little attention paid to traditional formats. Although most of the resources currently available are newsletters or tools for informal communication, that is changing quickly. The recent announcement that Medline will for the first time include indexing to an electronic journal is clear evidence that the distinction between Internet resources and other library resources is becoming less useful.

This change has many implications for the information professional. Databases are being developed by people who have little experience with library operations, and many of them are using protocols that are unique. As a result, patrons find that they must learn to cope with different conventions in virtually every file that they address. This makes it more difficult to find the best information to meet a specific need. As institutions provide more people access to these files by implementing "Gophers," distributing library databases through wide area networks (WAIS), and sharing electronic files through interinstitutional cooperatives, some patrons will need additional assistance. Falduto, Blythe, and McClure (1994) contend that the information professional must substitute an active partnership with researchers for a model of computer support that gives only policy guidance and technical support. Good service will be defined as service that provides access to information along with value-added services designed to facilitate its use (McLean 1994). The librarian clearly has a niche in this model. According to Grace Jackson-Brown (1993), the librarian will provide "a valuable conduit in the interdependent ecosystem that exists between information producers, researchers, and other information seekers" (p. 82).

Many campuses that provide excellent library reference services now connect people to the Internet with the proviso that they are on their own, but this is becoming less acceptable. As campuses come to rely more heavily on electronic datafiles as an information resource and as more students and other less sophisticated users gain better access to these systems, better services to users will be required at all levels. This will require unified service points where users can get help in understanding both the structure of the files being accessed and the means of delivery. If it is to be implemented, the distinction between the service mission of "library reference" that relates to the datafiles and "computer user services" that relates to the means of delivery will not be useful and must be discarded. Programs need to combine the kind of technical expertise now provided by computer professionals and the understanding of the content of files now available in traditional library service programs.

DEFINING THE PROBLEM

Questions arise as library professionals stretch their mission. How do libraries reach beyond the valuable service programs and collections that they have so carefully nurtured over the years to encourage the acceptance of new approaches to information delivery? How do they balance their investments so that they can both meet the needs of traditional users and deal with the demands of an increasingly sophisticated clientele? How do they identify and acquire the new technologies that their patrons require? How do they provide and coordinate the cluster of services in the library and beyond that make sense to a clientele that is addressing electronic and print resources with diverse sets of skills? How do they gain acceptance for those technologies among administrators who fund the library and among library patrons? How do libraries build the skill base within their workforce that is required to cope with new technologies when the skills we need are in short supply in librarianship, at a time when more people stay in their current positions for longer periods, and when many organizations are downsizing? Above all, how do libraries develop organizations that are innovative enough to meet the challenges at hand while staying within a budget?

BLENDING THE OLD AND THE NEW

There are no easy answers to any of these questions, and even fewer of the answers that might be offered are either permanent or have universal application. As libraries and related service organizations grapple with the questions being posed, transient solutions will have to be found that reflect local conditions, that take into account the starting point from which the organization addresses the questions, that use the skills that are available within the organization, or that can be purchased from the outside as new people are hired or from experts. Solutions must also reflect the personal preferences of those who administer the library, those who work there, those it serves, and those to whom the library reports. It is important that those who lead the library mold these preferences to meet modern realities. But a community of values must be developed among all of these groups, and library leaders cannot get so far ahead or behind that this community cannot be maintained. In all cases, individual libraries must learn to tailor their answers to the challenge posed by change to meet the specific condition of that library and its patrons.

The best organizational solutions that will be offered as the library works through this transition will have common characteristics. First, every successful solution will be based on more open communication within the library organization and between the library and others in the community in which it resides. It is critical that libraries acquire ideas for program development wherever they may be generated and provide the community they serve with information about changes in the resources available to them and in library programs as quickly as possible. This kind of communication requires the organization to be flexible enough to withstand criticism from all those who will use or will be asked to provide library services and to use the ideas generated through that criticism.

In addition, extraordinary efforts must be made to use the intellectual resources available to the library to best advantage. Cross-fertilization must be encouraged through wide-ranging discussions that include a variety of people who might not be used to working together. It is not enough for all communication to come through the hierarchy. Catalogers must talk to reference librarians, bibliographers and acquisitions librarians; librarians must talk to staff; library faculty and staff must talk to computer center personnel and audiovisual technicians; and users must be encouraged to offer suggestions and express their concerns about library services. In addition, all must be willing to hear what others have to say about the conflicting needs of delivering services to support a variety of functions on a static or dwindling budget.

Libraries must encourage risk taking among employees as it approaches innovation. As Keith Cottam (1989) put it, "Librarianship needs intrapreneurial managers and staff who are dreamers . . . people who can break with tradition and act to develop new roles and responsibilities, secure risk capital, co-opt emerging information technologies and develop new ones, and figure out new ways to make libraries essential in an information based society" (p. 523). Library managers must also be willing to accept some failures. This is not to say that resources can be wasted. The library must continue to focus on its mission and implement changes that reflect that mission. But the technological base of the library is changing rapidly enough that some choices that are made using the best information available will be outstripped by new developments before they are fully implemented. Library managers must reward those who are prepared to take calculated risks rather than punish them if those risks fail. Change and uncertainty must be viewed as constants. Card catalogs were forever; CD-ROM towers and OPACs are for five years.

ORGANIZING THE LIBRARY

The organizational structures of the library will also have to be adapted to its new situation. But it is not certain how radical or permanent these changes will or should be. In recent essays, Ann De Klerk and Joanne Euster (1989), Irene Hoadley (1994), and Patricia M. Larsen (1991) noted that most library organization charts still retain the kind of bureaucratic look that they have always had. This trend is not likely to reverse itself. Although it has been fashionable to criticize bureaucracy, this kind of structure has proven itself to be resilient even as its challengers come and go. Librarians are, in the main, comfortable with these structures, and career development in librarianship is based on the idea that people will move up the kind of organizational ladders that develop out of bureaus. In addition, many librarians fit within university organizations that are highly bureaucratized, and, in many cases, they are assigned these structures by administrators from outside the library. It is true that bureaucratic structures can make communications within the organization more difficult and retard change. But it has also been demonstrated that bureaus can be adapted to address these problems if they are well led.

Even though bureaucracies are likely to prevail in the library world, there are trends that seem to be appearing that are changing the way these bureaucracies operate. As Hoadley noted, more organizations are including more slots in their hierarchies for specialists who are expected to bring new talents and ideas to the operation. At the same time, libraries are decentralizing as organizations and more discrete boxes are being added to their organization charts to meet new demands for service. This kind of decentralization means that more first-level managers will have direct responsibility for a service area. Managers higher up the chain will have more of these units assigned to them and will be required to delegate more authority to those they supervise to run day-to-day operations.

Communications problems inherent in bureaucracies will have to be addressed in a variety of ways. Collegial relationships have been and are being used to ensure that information comes into the management system from all corners of the organization. Libraries have a long tradition of using extraorganizational committees and task forces to soften the edges of the boxes in their organizations. But they are increasingly finding that even this is not enough to meet the need for flexibility within their organizations. Planning programs will have to be developed that constantly look at the adequacy of programs and seek ways to correct their problems and update them.

It is also likely that the financial constraints facing libraries may actually help libraries address the need to flatten their structures and improve internal communications. As positions are cut for budgetary reasons without consideration of service needs, libraries will be forced to spend more of their money in direct service and less to support their administrative structures. The trend in industry to eliminate white-collar positions in an effort to increase productivity and the pressure within universities to put more people in the classroom will undoubtedly spill over into academic libraries. The result will be wider spans of control and fewer administrative tiers in library bureaus. Although this may be unsettling to some, it will clearly enhance the capacity of the organization to get input from users and make the library more responsive to its constituencies.

Some organizations have begun experimenting with team-based structures that are radically different from those in most libraries. These kinds of organizations are sometimes touted as providing more suitable working arrangements for professionals. They eliminate hierarchies and blur the distinction between librarians and others who work with them. This may or may not be the organization of the future (Riggs 1993).

But whether teams prevail or not, this approach to management will have an important influence on the way libraries organize themselves, particularly as it becomes more difficult to separate the "professionals" in the library from the "staff." This separation has never been easy, but as the skill base needed in the library expands to include people who can operate and repair electronic devices, it will become even more difficult.

This will be particularly true if universities choose to combine their information providers (to include media production and distribution, telephone services, networking, libraries, and computer personnel) into single units. The new organization that emerges will include professional staff whose job preparation is radically different from that of librarians and will alter the way information providers do business within the university community.

In any case, it is unlikely that library organizations will be as predictable as they have been in the past or that the graphic descriptions provided by their organization charts will be as consistent or as elegant. In fact, inelegance may emerge as a virtue as organizations grow organically. Joanne Euster (1992) speaks of organizations that are constantly becoming more complex and continuously changing in response to technology. This kind of organization consisting of bureaus with ill-defined and transitory territories is likely to be the rule in future libraries. Bureaus will be created to meet specific needs as they emerge, either because the organization is trying to learn a new task or to bring in new kinds of expertise. In some cases, these bureaus will become permanent. More often, this place on the chart will only survive so long as a specific person works in the library or until the desired skills can be learned and then dispersed throughout the structure. In either case, it is unlikely that changes in the chart will wait for a large-scale reorganization that will introduce a single, enduring, "best" scheme of organization to the library. Technology gives the manager more flexibility to rearrange library operations quickly as the need arises. But keeping up with change requires constant adjustment of the organization based on a planning process based on continuous review of the library and its program.

The reporting line of the library director may fall in any of three categories within the larger organizations in which he or she serves. Directors may continue to be charged only with the administration of the library under the charge of the office of academic affairs. They may find themselves with broader responsibilities, to include supervision of other information agencies on campus and report either to the president or the office of academic affairs. Or they may serve under a chief information officer who is neither a librarian or an academic. In any case, it is clear that this person will have to function as part of a more clearly defined team that includes members of the teaching faculty, the head of academic computing on campus, the chief telecommunications specialist, the network coordinator, and the audiovisual services unit. These elements must work together, and the competition that has existed between them for this turf must be eliminated if all are to prosper.

STAFFING THE LIBRARY

The role of the library professional will also change as the organization adapts to meet the changing needs of the library's clientele, and information professionals must also change if they are to cope with this new role. No matter what kind of organizational structure emerges, libraries will employ fewer librarians and more people with other kinds of training on their staffs. Many reference services have already begun to use support staff to screen reference questions, provide backup for clerical duties, answer frequently asked questions, and perform other tasks. Well-educated people always seem to be available for work in libraries, and these people can be trained locally to do much of the routine work in public service departments. Although professional librarians will still be needed to provide leadership for the library program by setting an appropriate tone for the service program, providing it with a philosophical base, training staff, connecting the library to "best practice" in the profession, and offering special skills to the patron, there is no doubt that more of the day-to-day work of the department can be shifted to paraprofessionals and other members of the support staff.

But there is also another reason that the ratio of librarians to other kinds of staff is likely to decline. As the role of the reference librarian changes from one of answering questions from reference books to interpreting various computer systems and networks to patrons, the library will have to include on its staff people with skills that have not previously been associated with librarianship. The introduction of microcomputers, OPACs, and CD-ROM networks has shown that it is useful to have full time technicians directly associated with reference units. As libraries move their CD-ROMs to wide area networks; make online circulation, data bases, and the card catalog available to their constituencies over phone lines; and begin to field questions relating to Internet, Freenets, and Gophers, new areas of expertise will be required that cannot currently be filled from within the ranks of librarianship. People with these skills may eventually emerge from library and information science programs. But it is unlikely that they will appear in critical mass in most libraries for the next ten years.

The presence of people with an aptitude for computing who have been trained locally to do the other things required of them in libraries will continue to grow as information gathering becomes more dependent on electronic devices. At the same time, it is likely that more of the areas that librarians have carved out for themselves that require them to use technology will pass to other members of the staff and faculty. For instance, it should be possible to teach people who have subject expertise in the sciences and who are facile with computers to perform high-quality brokered searches of specialized databases locally. Fewer, better prepared librarians will be required to train and supervise these workers and to ensure that quality is maintained. But it is clear that funding shortages, the difficulty of recruiting people with skills in the sciences, and questions of pure efficiency will lead to a time when this kind of task is passed to nonlibrarians.

If this kind of mixing of functions is to be accomplished, the library will have to develop the kind of job information family advocated by Anne Woodsworth and Theresa Maylone (1993). If libraries are to mix computer specialists with other staff and faculty, a mechanism must be developed that will allow the organization to determine the relative worth of these professionals in relation to other workers in the library and to compensate both traditional staff and computer specialists in an appropriate way. According to Woodsworth and Maylone, many of these people do similar jobs but are rewarded differently under current systems. The future success of libraries and the capacity of the university to integrate information-related activities may depend on the capacity of the organization to accomplish this kind of rationalization.

Libraries can also expect to have fewer full-time administrators in the future than they have become accustomed to. As noted earlier, the idea of providing managers with limited spans of control does not fit well into modern management theory, particularly as it relates to the management of professionals. At the same time, financial constraints are requiring organizations to cover more service programs with fewer people. In addition, it is becoming increasingly difficult to respond to changes in technology quickly unless decision makers are actively involved in programs using that technology. Just as in industry, libraries are finding that it is useful to operate their organizations with fewer supervisors and that organizations with fewer managers are more flexible than traditional organizations. As libraries begin to look at their productivity, fewer people will be working in management suites and more will be on the floor of the library.

Preparing librarians for work in the field also will present a challenge. The day of the generic librarian is gone. It is unlikely that library managers can expect to find new professionals who are prepared for both the immediate challenge of the job that they will face and the philosophical base that will fit them for a career. If they expect those entering librarianship to be able to grow into leadership roles in their organizations, they must recruit people with a broad-based appreciation of the complexities of the information environment. But, at the same time, libraries expect that new members of their professional staff come equipped with the basic skills required to perform the functional tasks associated with their first job. This may be too much to ask.

Master of Library Science (MLS) programs have not for some time been the place for librarians to learn "best practice." They are also not the place where librarians are taught to be library directors. It is illogical to expect that this will change. Librarians should expect to leave their MLS programs with a commitment to service, an appreciation of the principles on which the profession is built, some appreciation of the balance that must be struck between the needs for servicing traditional and electronic delivery systems for information, a minimal familiarity with organizations, and some potential to provide leadership in the field. Specific, job-related skills like cataloging, reference interview skills, computer literacy, management skills, and communications skills will have to be either prerequisites for entry into library school or, more likely, to be learned on the job.

For their own well-being, libraries must be prepared to hone the skills of any newcomer and to constantly update the skills of their staff and faculty to prepare them for additional responsibilities and the changing demands of their jobs. Libraries and other information organizations must also recognize that the skills and knowledge base of their profession is perishable. The organization must learn to import ideas from other libraries, from the community, and from the administration. It must also learn to develop those ideas quickly and systematically in a way that will allow them to be implemented with as little friction as possible. Scanning the environment for information that will have an impact on the library program must be continuous and must be a priority for everyone who works in the library if its leadership is to have the reaction time it needs to develop its program. At the same time, efforts to update and upgrade skill levels must also be constant to ensure that the library has the kind of personnel resources that it needs to do its job. This can only happen if everyone in the organization is charged with constantly evaluating what is being done and how it might be done better.

Professional development and programs designed to help both faculty and staff members learn new skills required on the job are no longer optional. It is no longer enough to expose faculty and staff to other professionals at library meetings or even to bring in occasional speakers. Libraries must develop targeted programs aimed at introducing the library staff to new ideas with the expectation that those ideas will become a part of the library program (Creth 1994).

Staff development affords the organization an opportunity to enhance its flexibility in changing times by reinforcing the idea that the library is willing to invest in its staff. Change is likely to be the only constant that we know in the information industry for a while. To cope with this kind of flux, staff must be open to change, and that openness must be achieved despite limited voluntary turnover in the staff. This requires a sense of community. Maintaining this sense of community within the organization can be difficult in a time of change. But it is important that the library make the people who have invested their lives in its program feel secure that there will always be a place for them. Efforts must be made to bring people together so that user concerns pass quickly to decision makers and so that solutions that respond to user needs are generated rapidly.

The library must also recognize that some of the specific tasks it performs, tasks that have been central to its mission throughout the years, may no longer be required. As a result, efforts must be made to retool and redirect valuable employees. Librarians and other staff members who envision careers of 30 or more years are going to have to be retrained several times before their careers end. For some, this will require only that they learn new techniques and skills to do what they have always done. But others will be asked to phase out jobs that they enjoy and value. The organization must take responsibility for insuring that every encouragement is given to those making these kinds of mid-career changes if the organization expects to keep pace with change. A climate must be created that supports the idea that retraining is a normal part of life that is to be expected, and an appropriate reward structure must be developed to support this idea. Encouraging people to believe that they are secure in the organization enhances their flexibility, and individual flexibility enhances the capacity of the library to respond to the changing dynamic of the library environment.

MAKING IT WORK—WHY THEY PAY MANAGERS THE BIG BUCKS

All of this leads to the conclusion that libraries face an exciting time. But they also face a time that is different from any that they have previously known. Librarians are a conservative lot, but they must learn to embrace technology and to change their organizations. The people who must develop service programs face the challenge of folding a group of people trained in a variety of eras into a unified service program that is in transition. Technologies will change more rapidly than staff, and some of those who are being asked to help patrons use that technology will be more interested in the new than will others. If the organization is to survive, managers must unite the staff behind a program that is evolving and build excitement about a future that is uncertain.

At the same time, those who provide funding for library programs must learn to look at budgeting for personnel and equipment in a different way. They must invest in constant staff development and learn to constantly depreciate old and phase in new equipment. Managers at all levels must learn to steer the organization in a way that will encourage innovation. They must also be willing to give their subordinates an opportunity to innovate on their own, and provide guidance when needed, but make correctives only when objectives are not being met. They must learn to encourage those who are willing to take risk, reassure those who are uncertain about the path that is being taken, and to be forceful with those who cannot bring themselves to make necessary changes. Above all, they must learn to minimize their own importance in the organization, stepping in when they are needed but staying out of the way when they are not.

Reference and other service programs will be different in the next century than they are now in both scope and content. It is the responsibility of the manager to maintain the commitment that libraries have always had to serve clients while discarding those preconceptions about staffing and expertise that will limit the library's capacity to meet the challenge presented by a changing environment. There will be friction, but good managers will use that friction creatively to add energy to their organizations and to induce appropriate changes. The key to the success of the library is finding managers for the profession who enjoy this challenge.

REFERENCES

Baker, Nicholson. 1994. "Discards." *The New Yorker* (April 4): 64–86.

Bergquist, William. 1993. *The Postmodern Organization: Mastering the Art of Irreversible Change.* San Francisco: Josey-Bass.

Bowen, William G. 1992. "Foreward." In Anthony M. Cummings et al., *University Libraries and Scholarly Communication: A Study Prepared for the Andrew W. Mellon Foundation.* Washington, DC: The Association of Research Libraries, 1992.

Cottam, Keith. 1989. "The Impact of the Library Intrapreneur on Technology." *Library Trends* 37: 521–531.

Creth, Sheila. 1994. "Changing Times: The Human & Organization Dimensions." Unpublished.

De Klerk, Ann, and Euster, Joanne R. 1989. "Technology and Organizational Metamorphoses." *Library Trends* 37: 157–168.

Euster, Joanne R. 1992. "The Impact on the Academic Library: Political Issues." In *Information Management and Organization Change in Higher Education: The Impact on Academic Libraries*, Gary M. Pitkin, ed. Westport, CT: Meckler.

Falduto, Ellen F., Blythe, Kenneth C., and McClure, Polley Ann. 1994. "The Information Age, the People Factor, and the Enlightened IS Manager." *Cause/Effect* 17 (Spring): 7–9.

Heterick, Robert C. 1993. "Introduction: Reengineering Teaching and Learning." In
    *Reengineering Teaching and Learning in Higher Education: Sheltered Groves,
    Camelot, Windmills, and Malls*. Boulder, CO: CAUSE.
Hoadley, Irene. 1994. "Somewhere Over the Rainbow: Organizational Patterns in Aca-
    demic Libraries." In *For the Good of the Order: Essays in Honor of Edward G.
    Holley*, Delmus E. Williams et al., eds. Westport, CT: JAI Press.
Jackson-Brown, Grace. 1993. "The Academic Librarian's New Role as Information
    Provider." *Reference Librarian* 39: 77–83.
Larsen, Patricia. 1991. "The Climate of Change; Library Organizational Structures,
    1985–1990." *Reference Librarian* 37: 79–93.
Lowry, Anita. 1994. "The Information Arcade, University of Iowa Libraries." In *Man-
    aging Information Technology as a Catalyst of Change: Proceedings of the 1993
    CAUSE Annual Conference, December 7–10, San Diego, California*. Boulder,
    CO: CAUSE.
Lynch, Beverly P. 1978. "Libraries as Bureaucracies." *Library Trends* 26: 259–267.
McLean, Neil. 1994. "The Management of Information Access in Higher Education."
    Cause/Effect 17 (Spring): 43–46.
Moran, Barbara. 1994. "What Lies Ahead for Academic Libraries? Steps on the Way to
    the Virtual Library." In *For the Good of the Order: Essays in Honor of Edward
    G. Holley*. Delmus E. Williams et al., eds. Westport, CT: JAI Press.
Riggs, Donald E. 1993. "Managing Quality: TQM in Libraries." *Library Administration
    & Management* 7 (Spring): 73–78.
Woodsworth, Anne, and Maylone, Theresa. 1993. *Reinvesting in the Information Job
    Family: Context, Changes, New Jobs, and Models for Evaluation and Compen-
    sation*. Boulder, CO: CAUSE.

6 Preparing for the Technological Future

Charles B. Lowry

It is generally accepted that libraries are going through a transition that is transforming them dramatically. This transformation is very much like the one they went through a century ago when the current paradigm was established (Lowry 1993). Like that transition, the current one is driven by technology. Our response to the difficulty of this change ought to be that we experiment vigorously with new services and technologies, making the shift toward those that have the promise of providing information resources for the future. Several critical areas will influence what we do and the strategies we adopt. We must formulate a vision that will result in a foundation for the virtual library that is as good as the old paradigm. That is primarily a problem of logical thinking, keeping in mind the central premise that we are in the business of providing information, not in providing information technology nor preserving libraries as we know them.

Two basic tasks must be accomplished to build the virtual library infrastructure, and neither is trivial. The first is to build a foundation of information technologies (IT) that allows users to access electronic information easily, seamlessly—and without becoming technology experts. The second is to create a substantial amount of digitized scholarly information that users really want to use. This chapter is devoted to addressing only the first set of problems and preparing for the technological future. However, much of this work will support the second task, which is the work of publishers—including commercial and university presses, scholarly associations and secondary publishers. The networked environment will also stimulate much entrepreneurial experimentation with electronic publishing.

The principal themes of this chapter fall into three topical areas. First is the software and hardware IT infrastructure, which is the prerequisite for the virtual library. Here, the keys to the technological future are distributed computing and networking; open architectures and standards; authentication, authorization, and encryption; and billing and royalty tracking. Second, there are fundamental problems for information retrieval (IR) that must be solved to create the technology needed to make IR viable in the distributed full-text future. Call this the virtual library tool kit—it will include reduced dependence on word indexing and keyword/Boolean retrieval; the development and broad application of natural language processing (NLP); and effective tools for navigation of the network, which are based on good human factors work on human computer interaction (HCI). Third, Carnegie Mellon University offers some helpful examples of how IT and IR can be used to build the virtual library. This chapter concludes with some brief illustrations of efforts that exploit this new computing environment including work on graphical user interface, full-text journals on the campus network, NLP of full text files, and digital archiving of historical materials.

INFORMATION TECHNOLOGY INFRASTRUCTURE

Identifying the key technologies that will reshape the library paradigm does not require comprehensive understanding of the details of new technological applications in computing and telecommunications. Rather, it is a function of understanding the opportunities for transformation of scholarly information within the computing and telecommunications context and of establishing a set of technology requirements that will answer the needs of libraries as information mediators.

Distributed Computing Architectures

There is great promise in the emerging distributed architecture and complex file systems to build a new medium for scholarly information. Understanding this basic framework is the essential task for creating electronic libraries. In the early 1980s, distributed computing was a new area in which many problems were recognized but few were solved. By the middle of the decade, basic solutions were emerging not only in the commercial sector but also in universities, with projects like Andrew at Carnegie Mellon University and Athena at the Massachusetts Institute of Technology (MIT). Today the fruits of those ten years of labor have reached a stage where commercialization is making distributed computing affordable and, in effect, inevitable. The essence of distributed processing is that computing resources at different locations are interconnected over networks so that computing resources and—more importantly to us—information may be shared.

There are several economic factors that make the use of distributed processing compelling. First and foremost is that the cost of computers has continued to drop exponentially. Small processors are becoming easily affordable even for individuals. This trend has reversed an accepted rule known as Grosch's law which states that the "cost per machine instruction executed . . . [is] . . . inversely proportional to the square of the size of the machine" (Martin 1982: 23). In effect, the millions of instructions per second (MIPS) needed for modern data processing can be achieved more cheaply by distributing computing functions across smaller machines than by using larger ones. A simple, local example is illustrative. At Carnegie Mellon University, we have improved the performance of our online catalog by producing two copies running on different machines. This also allows for increased simultaneous use.

There are several other cost factors that are closely related to the development of distributed computing. Technology is reducing costs of data transmission. Development of networks is improving access to networks nationwide, driven by both the government and commercial sectors. Closely allied with computing costs is the decline in cost for storage and the development of new storage media. This is reinforced by the development of high-volume applications in areas like banking, marketing, entertainment, airline reservations, newswire services, security information, and other continuous streaming data. These high-volume applications lower the cost for applications of more direct interest to libraries, that is, those related to scholarship (Martin 1981: 2–19).

At Carnegie Mellon University, the "computing paradigm envisioned in Andrew is a marriage between personal computing and time-sharing. It incorporates the flexibility and visually rich user-machine interface made possible by the former, with the ease of communication and information sharing characteristic of the latter" (Morris 1986: 185). The Andrew Project's successes can be summed up in two words, scale and diversity of the application. "Never before has there been an attempt to support so many autonomous computers, each under the control of an unconstrained, untrained individual. Reliability, performance, and usability requirements conspire to make the design of such a system an intellectual challenge of the first magnitude" (Morris 1986: 200). The state of the art was advanced in several areas by Carnegie Mellon's Andrew Project: (1) machine-independent raster graphics; (2) large, secure, distributed file systems; (3) ubiquitous, high-performance text editing; and (4) mail and bulletin board systems. In the Andrew System, Carnegie Mellon University Libraries had a unique opportunity, which was fulfilled by the Mercury Project and the development of the Library Information System (LIS). It is worth mentioning that the objectives of the Andrew Project were similar to those of the Athena Project at MIT, which began somewhat later, specifically "the support of Educational Computation, especially for undergraduates. This computational support was intended for all students, not just Science and Engineering" (Champine 1991: 12).

The commercialization of the Andrew distributed computing environment was one of the initial goals established by Carnegie Mellon University's Information Technology Center and its partner, IBM. Transarc Corporation is commercializing the Andrew File System (AFS) under the name Distributed File System (DFS). DFS has been accepted by the Open Software Foundation as a standard for their distributed computing environment. Indeed, Carnegie Mellon University is in the midst of the implementation of Transarc's DFS. With it will come significant improvements in modularity, which will result in better system dependability. Most importantly, this time around, the system will be characterized by stronger support for major commercial workstations produced by Apple and IBM, although the UNIX workstation support will remain a key element. In this new environment, file services will be provided by DFS. The Macintosh groups will continue to use AppleShare and PC groups will use netware from Novell. The end result will be better integration of three quite different environments, and the improvement of interoperability of systems campus-wide. DFS will be used widely to integrate computing environments in business and education. Thus, the Carnegie Mellon experience is a good example of the opportunities and problems presented by distributed computing architectures and has resulted in the availability of important technologies to be applied elsewhere.

Open Architectures and Standards

At the dawn of distributed computing, around 1980, it was observed that "there will be incompatibility problems in distributed processing networks between machines of different manufacturers for a long time to come. The machines may be interconnectable . . . but not capable of being generally *bound*. . . . Process-to-process communication will then have to take place by sending transactions from one incompatible machine to another, as on Arpanet, rather than the tighter coupling of DECnet or SNA. There is hope, however, that standard protocols for terminal access and file access will emerge" (Martin 1981: 554). If this set of problems had persisted, the development of distributed architectures would have been dramatically inhibited due to proprietary hardware and software standards, and the promise of distributed digital libraries would not now be achievable. However, by the middle of the 1980s, the development of standards was vigorously underway and much of the open systems interconnection envisioned in the OSI reference model was in place with ISO standards before 1990 (RMG Consultants 1992: 2).

Among the most important actions we can take as librarians in the current environment, is to make a strident demand that vendors adhere to the principles of open systems. For hardware vendors, this means avoiding proprietary operating systems that are incompatible with standards like ANSI C, Berkeley UNIX, and DFS. To the library automation vendors, this means adherence to standards established by Z39. In an environment like Andrew at Carnegie Mellon or Athena at MIT, interoperability and coherence mean "that the same application source code, and most of the system source code, can be compiled and executed on all workstations regardless of architecture" (Champine 1991: 93). Industry-wide standards are important also for small system storage technology and retrieval, as any librarian who has tried to install a CD network will attest. If providers would all use standard query language, standard storage formats, and standard protocols, then users would not be forced to adapt to a variety of interfaces. Moreover, we would be able to improve access to dedicated CD LANs by developing campus-wide access.

Across wide-area networks, however, compatibility presents additional problems. "Various levels of system compatibility are possible, including the binary level, execution level, and protocol level" (Champine 1991: 89). Not even the hardware of a single vendor successfully supports all compatibility at the binary level. Systems like Athena and Andrew support compatibility at the execution level. It is at the protocol level that network compatibility will be achieved. Open systems will mean that software applications are portable and that vendor hardware is interoperable. The open systems interconnection reference model with its seven layers will ensure that "queries, results, and diagnostic and control information have been transferred between machines in a mutually comprehensible way according to mutually understood sequences" (RMG Consultants 1992: 1–2). In this instance, of course, understanding means machine understanding.

The Z39.50 standard operates in the top application layer of the OSI model. "Z39.50 is the best technology we have today to present a single user interface to access the multiplicity of information resources on a network. Virtually all Z39.50 implementations are running over TCP/IP—not OSI. There is no OSI network" (RMG Consultants 1992: 6). "A mechanism is provided by Z39.50 through which the sharing of bibliographic, full-text, and image data could radically change the way libraries interact. For years we have talked about the library without walls, and this development could certainly be key to that concept" (MacKinnon et al. 1993: 237). Conformance to the standard means that it would be possible to implement clients and servers from "different vendors with different operating systems (e.g., UNIX, Next, Motif, Windows, NT) and different hardware platforms (e.g., 486-class and greater Intel-based PCs; H-P, Sun, Next, and DEC Alpha, AXP, etc. workstations) would offer a choice of different technical environments, and a choice of user interfaces" (RMG Consultants 1992: 10).

However, implementing the ANSI/NISO standard Z39.50 is neither straightforward nor a trivial task. In the first place, the standard is not complete and there are significant questions that must be answered. For instance, "an area that still awaits resolution by the community of implementers concerns the mapping of queries. Because systems have indexed similar types of data differently, a search entered on one system may not yield the expected results when carried out on another system" (Stovel et al. 1993: 229). Local implementations may also have idiosyncratic characteristics to cover local needs or to fill gaps left by the standard. For example, chemical formulas are represented in the Research Libraries Information Network (RLIN) system in a format specific to Engineering Index Page (EIP) and not standard to USMARC. These representations will be translated by another system's Z39.50 implementation in variable ways, none of which represent the chemical formula (MacKinnon et al. 1993: 234).

Similarly, use of the Z39.58 search syntax could lead to difficulties. For instance, in the Carnegie Mellon University LIS client, the standard syntax "AU" for author also represents the chemical symbol for gold and a French preposition. This results in the retrieval of nearly 12,000 records with those terms in various databases of LIS. Finding the journal title *Au Courant* will be impossible for many users. Similar problems occur with syntax "TI" for title, which also means titanium, a musical note, a tree type, and an Italian word. The explanation for this problem is that "Z39.58 requires that two-letter index abbreviations (without punctuation) precede keywords (e.g., AU Smith). Therefore, any two-letter words, abbreviations, acronyms, etc., which match the index designations cannot be searched unless they appear in quotation marks" (Troll, *Search Syntax* 1993: 1–2). This is an example of the way in which standards can converge with client design and the application of vendor-provided software (in this case, Fulcrum and Newton) to create serious problems that have to be resolved, either by programmers or by librarians instructing users. These problems not withstanding, the implementation of open systems and accepted standards remains our best hope for improving information services in the electronic environment.

Authentication, Authorization, and Encryption

The creation of a national distributed network based on open systems and the application of standards brings us to the third hurdle in the creation of virtual library domains. This is the protection of intellectual property rights and privacy in the electronic environment. The attendant techno-logical problems are authentication, authorization, and encryption. Authentication ensures that users on the systems are who they say they are; authorization ensures appropriate access to authenticated users; and encryption protects the privacy of users and the integrity of data being transmitted over a network.

Security and privacy are important because many people in many places have access to a computer network. The information shared in some of the network machines may be of great value to a corpo-ration. It must not be lost, stolen, or damaged. It is important to protect the data and programs from hardware and software failures from catastrophes and from criminals, vandals, incompetence, and people who will misuse it.

A network is often shared by users for whom security is of little or no importance, and users for whom it is vital. It may be shared by users who are highly responsible with urgent business and others who are irresponsible and likely to try anything (Martin 1981: 517).

There are five essential issues that relate to network security: (1) users should be identifiable; (2) users actions must be authorized and monitored; (3) data hardware and software must be protected from harm and unauthor-ized use; (4) data must be reconstructable, auditable, and tamper proof; and (5) transmission over the network must be fail-safe and private.

Cryptography is an ancient art that has been dramatically changed by electronic technology. In simplest terms, the safe scheme uses both a complex algorithm and a crypto key, which is a "random collection of bits or characters which the transmitting and receiving stations use in conjunction with the algorithm for enciphering and deciphering. If the enemy knows the algorithm but not the crypto key, it would take a large amount of work for him to break the code" (Martin 1981: 529; see also, Salton 1989: 131–58). For instance, a key of 80 bits would take more time than the age of the universe to decipher (Martin: 1981: 530).

Within the Andrew System at Carnegie Mellon, Kerberos, the authentication scheme developed in MIT's Athena project has been implemented. This is a "trusted, third-party, private key, network authentication system that validates the identity of individuals to network servers" (Champine 1991: 92). It is important to remember that in the distributed environment workstations are unlikely to be secure, and it is therefore necessary to have security built into the network itself. Client users and the network server have encryption keys, and time stamps have also been implemented to prevent replay of keys captured by eavesdroppers on the network who wish to use them illegally.

Kerberos operates without any further burden on the individual user once they have logged onto the system. When a user seeks access to the Andrew System, they must provide the authentication service with a unique ID and a password not only common to the individual but to the authentication server. They are issued an electronic ticket, which is passed to the servers whenever a client requests access to a database service (Champine 1991: 92–93, 98–99, 124–28)—for instance, a licensed database on the Library Information System. Our LIS authentication has been successfully merged with the Andrew System authentication and that of the School of Computer Science, both of which are Kerberos based but are integrated into the respective computer environments differently. The user who is already logged on to one of the systems may run LIS without additional authentication.

Authorization of an authenticated user to gain access to a particular database is part of our name service, which uses the Andrew File System implemented on a number of other campuses, including MIT. Within the Andrew File System, a name service functions to map database names to network addresses so that LIS users will be routed, without effort, to the correct retrieval server on which a database resides. The user is then connected. This information about the location of LIS servers is dynamically transmitted to the user's client or workstation. A near-term goal is to build a reference server and to move all the name services to the server side, eliminating this work from the user's workstation. This will give us flexibility to build user interfaces on a number of different client architectures and is similar to the name service Hesiod, developed in Project Athena (Champine 1991: 129–32). It bears repeating that the essence of authorization is that it allows authenticated users access only to information to which they have a right. Anyone who telnets to LIS will be allowed access to our locally owned databases but, without proper authentication, they cannot look at databases that we license from companies like Information Access Corporation and University Microfilms International.

Billing and Royalty Tracking

In the contemporary information landscape, a number of factors limit what we can accomplish in directing this process of change. Libraries will not have large amounts of new resources to buy electronic information or information technology, although it is not a zero-sum game. Publishers and other suppliers of information may emphasize the "value added" by electronic information, but it will not alter this basic fact. Document delivery to end-users is one essential part of the information services equation that libraries provide, but there is little reason to believe that there is a large, highly profitable and untapped market of end-users that will become available to publishers of electronic information, which is today distributed in printed books and journals.

Like many things in life, economics will dictate how long it takes to have the bulk of scholarly information available electronically as a primary medium of publishing. As the networked infrastructure has been built, we have not seen a sudden and large-scale shift to its use for delivery by scholarly publishers because of the question of security. The economics of book and journal publishing in the print environment, although not totally secure, are well known and the methods for ensuring profitability of publication are clear (White 1993: 295–96). Publishing of scholarly information is international in scope and will require a period of transition before publishers can eliminate traditional print publication, simply because the information technology infrastructure will have an uneven development internationally. We must work from analogies that are implicit in the old paradigm to inform the future and to guide us in constructing relationships that will work best for libraries, publishers, and vendors in the new electronic network.

Billing and royalty tracking is an emerging issue for electronic publishing in both the local campus environment and at the "macro" level on the Internet. This problem must be solved to facilitate the rapid shift to electronic publication. There are several ways to do it, and the most commonly used is site licensing. Each of the databases available through

LIS at Carnegie Mellon is licensed for use in our campus environment. Authentication gives us the control to honor licensing requirements of this type, but authentication is only a necessary first step to remunerate publishers in this manner. An alternative is payment per use.

For instance, Carnegie Mellon University Libraries has just released the new Electronic Journal Article Delivery Service (E-JADS) to the system. E-JADS is a pilot service developed with University Microfilms International (UMI) that exploits CD-ROM-based journal images. The image documents on CD-ROM are linked to searches in LIS for Periodical Abstracts and ABI/INFORM. If a user retrieves a journal citation for which we have the image, they are reminded of the service and can order a laser-printed copy online. This is an intermediate step to distributing journal images across the campus network for display on workstations. The user is obligated to come to the library to pick up a copy and pay for it. This is similar to UMI's stand-alone Proquest service.

Local billing is a standard and fairly manageable technological problem, although it requires some fairly sophisticated work including authentication. Billing and royalty tracking on wide area networks such as the Internet is quite another matter. At the present time, this is accomplished by service providers within their own environments. Libraries have been paying for search services and cataloging charges with monthly bills for a long time. More recently, some innovation has crept in with the introduction of the use of credit cards for library-type services such as CARL'S Uncover database. In the future, none of this will satisfy the basic need to charge even in very small increments for the use of information. As an extreme example, let us suppose a library user in Pittsburgh has been routed from their library's online system through the Internet to a server that provides basic information in page format. Further, let us assume that the print charge is $0.10 per page. It seems unlikely that an information provider would be able to sustain an effective business sending out bills for a dime. Thus, there are a good number of commercial and private enterprises that would wish to provide information services through the Internet, but are prevented from doing so because of the technological complexity and expense of billing. On the other hand, users of information—whether libraries or individuals— are faced with the inhibiting effect of receiving many bills for different individual services.

The answer to this dilemma is a full-blown Internet billing service (IBS) designed as a centralized entity, which will provide billing and directory services for information companies. Information providers would be able to provide access to large databases even at small incremental charges while the benefit to the user would be a single consolidated bill and access to a directory of available services. The basic requirements of an IBS are (1) cross-realm authentication and communication; (2) account management for service providers and end-users; (3) billing and statement generation; (4) auditable accounting and financial reporting; (5) transaction handling including authorization to services and payment guarantee; and (6) directory services, that is, yellow pages. As it happens, some work has already been done to design the architecture and develop a running prototype at Carnegie Mellon by our Information Networking Institute. This "MS4 Billing Server" had several important design goals:

- *Extensibility*—Although the design is based on a reduced set of requirements, it should be easily expandable without a major revision of the design.
- *Simplicity*—Simplicity at the interface between a service providers server and the billing server. Service providers should not have to make major changes to their servers in order to utilize the billing server.
- *Security*—The transaction protocols must protect both end-user and service provider. The service provider must be guaranteed payment for rendered services, while the end-user must be guaranteed established prices.
- *Minimal communications*—Minimal communications with the billing server during a service transaction. The protocol should be designed to minimize the bottleneck at the billing server (Bodner et al. 1993: 2–4).

An Internet billing service something like the MS4 billing server will have to be implemented to ensure the broadest possible application of commercially published information in a networked environment.

VIRTUAL LIBRARY TOOL KIT

So far, this chapter has touched primarily on the technological infrastructure that will support a networked environment in which virtual libraries may be developed. The next level of concern is technologies which are used directly for IR, what might be called the "virtual library tool kit."

Keyword/Boolean Methods—Retrieval and Linguistic Problems

Today there are literally thousands of databases available on servers over the Internet and commercial networks worldwide. "These retrieval services all use conceptually similar methodologies, usually based on dense inverted indexes representing all term assignments to the records" (Salton 1989: 364). "Electronic storage and retrieval of information was the result of two major achievements: the advancement of computer technology, initiated to a large extent by the works of an American scientist, Claude Shannon, in 1938, and the development of the principles of coordinate indexing and retrieval by an American team headed by Mortimer Taube in 1951. Both of these achievements are based on, and are the application of, the theoretical work of an Englishman, George Boole, whose writings date back to 1854" (Smith 1993: 225).

The predominant form of information storage and retrieval technologies has been based on binary algebra and Boolean logic using three operators, "or," "and," and "not." In simplest terms, a descriptor's presence in a document determines if it will or will not be retrieved (Salton 1989: 231–33). The predominance of this form of IR is a testimony to just how difficult the problem of machine retrieval of information really is. The failures of keyword/Boolean techniques are well known, yet nothing has taken their place. I believe that they will fail us utterly as an increasing amount of the information we need for library services is available only or primarily on servers. Salton, in his classic text, put it this way: "The Boolean formulations cannot easily be related to particular desired output sizes. When the queries are broadly formulated with 'or' operators, a large output set may overwhelm the user. On the other hand, narrowly formulated queries using 'and' operators may generate very little output. In general, formulating useful Boolean queries is an art that is not accessible to uninitiated users" (Salton 1989: 236). Yet we have seen keyword and Boolean systems implemented in virtually all competitive library OPACs.

Over the years, two main measures of retrieval effectiveness have been used consistently. Recall is defined as the proportion of relevant materials retrieved from a corpus, and precision is the proportion of retrieved materials that are actually relevant to the question. One consistent feature of the empirical tests on IR systems is that high precision at, say, 80 percent results in low recall of relevant documents, less than 20 percent. The reverse is also true (Salton 1989: 278). These results are validated time and again. For instance, Blair and Maron, using the IBM STAIRS system for legal documentation, "showed its retrieval effectiveness to be surprisingly poor . . . on average recall of 20% and precision of 79%" (Blair and Maron 1985: 289, 293; see also McKinin et al. 1991: 297–307). Low recall values in current full-text retrieval systems occur because their "design is based on the assumption that it is a simple matter to foresee the exact words and phrases that will be used in the documents they will find useful, and only in those documents. This assumption is not a new one; it goes back over 25 years to the early days of computing. . . . Experiments show that full-text retrieval has worked well only on unrealistically small databases" (Blair and Maron 1985: 295).

Given these facts, it is somewhat ironic that one of the methods for improving the retrieval results users obtain in online catalogs is by the addition of text information in various forms such as tables of contents and abstracts (see Dillon and Wenzel 1990; Van Orden 1990; and Byrne and Micco 1988). As Dillon points out, "The addition of content-bearing information in bibliographic records will improve the overall retrieval effectiveness of library catalogs. However, the improvement is primarily in terms of recall. Precision will suffer as more content-bearing information is added to records" (Dillon and Wenzel 1990: 45–46).

One thing is certain. We are at the beginning of a transition from print to electronic information, the speed of which will be determined by many variables. Among the most serious inhibiting factors is the inability of current retrieval systems to allow users to recover relevant text with high precision. The essence of the problem is that keyword and Boolean retrieval from word-based indexes to full-text just cannot stand up to the rigorous demands that will be placed on them by large databases of text in machine readable form. There are four basic linguistic problems that underlie this failure:

- *Different words–same meaning*—Word-based processing fails to capture the variation in expression associated with synonymy, general/technical usage distinctions, and domain-specific idiom. For example, stomach pain after eating versus postprandial abdominal discomfort or tummy ache.

- *Same words–different meaning*—Word-based processing cannot readily accommodate the differences signaled by natural-language syntax. For example, Venetian blind versus blind Venetians and building code problems with development projects versus building projects with code development problems.

- *Pragmatic perspective–circumlocution*—Word-based processing does not control for differences in perspective that different users may bring to an information searching task. For example, lawyers on opposite sides of a damage case may regard an event—and refer to it consistently—from individual perspective; the accident versus the unfortunate incident.

- *Domain specificity*—Word-based processing cannot handle the sense restriction typical of language in domain-specific usage. For example, floating has different senses in banking and in swimming; sharp is principally a pain-sensation modifier in clinical medicine; secondarily, a measure of mental acuity—and unrelated to your kitchen paring knife.

In addition, there is the problem of language "confusability," which has been well documented in research:

- Each person will think of five ± two terms for an "information object."
- The chances that one person's "most favored term" will equal another's are about one in six.
- The chances that one person's five terms will include one of another person's five are about one in two.
- 100 people will come up with 30 names for an "object."

The full-text problems of academic and research libraries are both near term and long term:

- *Immediately*—We need to make various kinds of information available and accessible: library catalogs, databases of surrogate information in journals owned by the library, full-text reference works, campus information, university technical reports, other full-text intellectual properties, and individually provided documents.
- *In the near future*—We need to cope with (organize, access, navigate) enormous volumes of information: full-text journal articles, statistical information, technical information (including images), multiple media, remote databases and information systems, increasing quantities of scanned and other electronic materials (CLARITECH Corporation, December 1993: 12–13).

Natural Language Processing—Breakthrough Technology

So, what tools do we have that answer this increasing demand for good retrieval from electronic full-text? Recently a new phrase has crept into the lexicon—"natural language processing" (see Tenopir 1993; Pritchard-Schoch 1993; Quint 1993). NLP has the potential to answer many of the key problems. Carnegie Mellon University Libraries have formed a partnership with our computational linguistics group, which developed an NLP software system. Known as CLARIT, it is currently being commercialized. We are already in the process of applying CLARIT software technology to library domains (Figure 6.1).

CLARIT stands for Computational Linguistic Approaches to the Retrieval and Indexing of Text—that is, the application of techniques from computational linguistics to improve information management.

The essential features of the CLARIT approach include

Figure 6.1
CLARIT™ Indexing and Retrieval

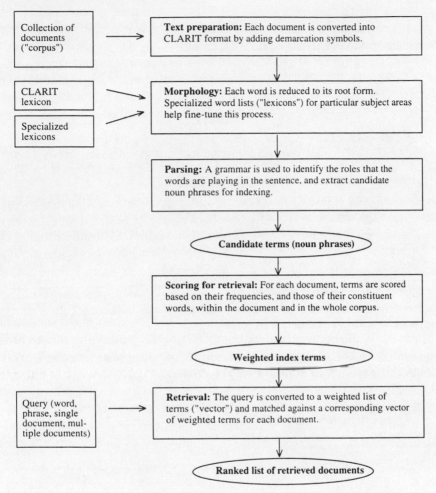

Published with permission of CLARITECH Corporation, 319 South Craig St., Pittsburgh, PA 15213.

- The use of selective natural-language processing to identify linguistic phrases as information units; and
- The use of empirically grounded thesauri to guide the selection and weighting of terms for document indexing and filtering.

CLARIT is a set of software tools for managing the information contained in large collections of electronic documents that supports work with collections by automatically characterizing their content and topical organization, profiling individual documents, and providing sophisticated methods for finding documents relevant to a particular topic. CLARIT goes beyond the capability of most current commercial systems in a number of ways. CLARIT is

- *Flexible*—It can work with almost any kind of electronic text, including technical articles and abstracts, libraries of patents and "prior art" libraries, electronic mail messages, unstructured historical archives, and news articles that are arriving over a network.
- *Fully automatic*—It discovers for itself all the information it needs to process documents. It doesn't require special knowledge resources such as vocabulary lists, semantic nets, or topic clusters.
- *Fast*—It can process more than a million documents overnight, and then compile in real time a list of documents relevant to a query.
- *Precise*—It has unusually high precision when retrieving documents. Most of the documents it finds are relevant to the query topic on the first try.
- *Easy to use*—It doesn't require a special query language. Queries can be expressed using plain English.

It is beyond the scope of this discussion to give a detailed assessment of the linguistic applications within the CLARIT technology. CLARIT is one of several advanced systems using linguistic approaches to IR problems. "The techniques that are employed are designed to be generalizable to many domains and scalable to large databases. Based on the observation that searching is done to obtain facts, and most facts are expressed in terms of noun phrases, CLARIT NLP processing is designed to identify candidate noun phrases in free text and to map them into index terms" (Hersh et al. 1992: 1402–03).

There are a number of arguments for basing IR technologies on phrases. Phrases approximate concepts more closely than words in isolation or in Boolean combination. The results of the most advanced evaluations, the Text REtrieval Conference-I and the Text REtrieval Conference-II (TREC) (see Harman 1993; Harman forthcoming), confirm this projection in large measure. Although it is difficult to make cross-system comparisons based on performance in TREC-processing tasks, the systems that consistently showed the lowest precision and recall were those using traditional word indexing based on keyword and Boolean retrieval strategies. The systems that showed the highest precision and recall used "advanced" IR techniques, including vector-space modeling in combination with sophisticated term weighting. CLARIT was one of the best performing systems, and the only one that also employed full NLP.

Sponsored by National Institute of Standards and Technology (NIST) and Advanced Research Projects Agency (ARPA), the TREC evaluations are the only standardized basis on which comparisons of this type have been made. The large-scale task required at TREC was processing of over 1 million documents with scientifically designed measures to compare the results (CLARITECH Corporation, December 1993: 91–99). Thus, there is already strong empirical evidence that good natural language processing software is the breakthrough technology required to effectively manage large amounts of full-text information, which will characterize the new electronic library environment. We expect to have pretype tests in 1994, and general application in three years or less using CLARIT NLP.

Tunneling, Surfing, Navigating—Is the Internet Ready?

In some measure, we have "crammed" automation down the throats of library patrons as a by-product of technical services activities, although with very good intentions. "Because much of the hard work in the early implementation stages was on the technical services side . . . , it was perhaps natural that reference librarians . . . were not counted among those most responsible for bringing forward the technology in libraries" (Nielsen and Baker 1987: 571). But we have now begun to take hold of events and are consciously and deliberately starting to shape automation to the human needs of our patrons.

As we begin to exploit the Internet, we must keep in mind two salient facts—it is really just a large distributed computing system with a decentralized administration, which makes it enormously complex and difficult to make "user-friendly," and it will become a preeminent feature of the virtual library. The use of the Internet within the new library paradigm will result from two sets of efforts—the work of individual librarians as experts who will guide library patrons toward resources that are useful for their particular information needs and the integration of Internet resources within the libraries' information technology environment. The Internet presents many problems to the common user. Resources available are diverse, difficult to find, and extremely uneven, so much so that the best advice a reference librarian currently might give a typical undergraduate is not to bother if they want authoritative information.

Nonetheless, it is useful for librarians to plunge ahead with the work of learning the Internet—including managers, who must have some minimum perspective on what it provides. Those responsible for library information services and information technology must maintain a level of understanding well beyond this. "Most people don't get really excited about having a guaranteed bit stream between machines, no matter how fast the lines or exotic the technology that creates it. They want to use that bit stream to do something useful, whether that is to move a file, access some data, or play a game" (Krol 1992: 25). In a mock look back from the year 2000, Dave Barry recently poked fun at the Information Superhighway: "The problem, of course, was that even though the information was coming a lot faster, the vast majority of it, having originated with human beings, was still wrong" (Barry 1994: 53). The question of the volume and quality of information is a critical one for publishers and librarians.

However, the plain fact is that the technology is also problematic. In spite of the serious and sustained effort to provide better interface tools for the user, we are a long way from a good common user interface. Perhaps that is why metaphors like tunneling, surfing, and navigating are typically used to describe the current state of the art. The developers of tools to exploit Internet resources have adopted the advanced client/server model of computing. Moreover, to a great extent, each new interface tool has built on its predecessors. Current Internet technologies like Gopher, WAIS, and WWW have been designed to explore distributed resources, but they have several serious limitations. First, they depend on keyword/Boolean retrieval, which is difficult to use and inadequate for full-text information retrieval. Second, they provide no consistent organizational structure or visual aids to help users keep track of where they are or what resources they have explored. This lack of context burdens short term memory and interfaces with scholarly work (see Hansen and Haas 1988). Third, the authority of current Internet resources is suspect; there is no way to distinguish between superior and inferior information. Fourth, the current software does not organize and facilitate access to Internet resources based on subject or content. That users need and expect access to intellectual content is apparent in the library literature (see Ahrens and Esquer 1993; Byrne and Micco 1988).

One of the earliest problems on the Internet was locating software resources by means other than interpersonal networking, which grows progressively more inefficient as the resources in a distributed network grow larger. Archie clients and servers were developed to fill this need. They are designed for locating anonymous FTP software and other files publicly available on the network. Searching with Archie is functionally dependent on file names and keyword indexes provided by the managers of these services (Krol 1992: 155, 162).

The Gopher service was developed to look up Internet resources using menus, connect to those resources, and use them in a fairly seamless fashion. The advantages are clear—the user does not have to look up addresses or names for servers and use Telnet commands to get to them. Because Gopher is a top-level tool, users will find resources represented in highly differential ways once they make connections, since there are no standard ways of organizing Gopher servers (Krol 1992: 189–91).

WAIS is another relatively new tool for gaining access to Internet resources that have been indexed by the service providers. Indexes may be provided in a number of ways—automatically using computer-generated word indexes or by the use of authority-based indexing—and databases may be virtually any kind of file. WAIS, like Gopher, allows the user to retrieve information from any public server on the network. Unlike Gopher, it is not menu-driven but retrieves information based on a word description and the various server locations where the user told it to look. In addition, WAIS is one of the most important tools that is Z39.50 compliant. Finally, it provides normalized scores for documents, which it returns to the user (Krol 1992: 211–13).

World-Wide Web is the most recently developed technology for users of the Internet and is based on hypertext technology. WWW "is a way of viewing all the online information available on the Internet as a seamless, browsable continuum. Using hypertext jumps and searches, the user navigates through an information world partly hand-authored, partly computer-generated from existing databases and information systems. The Web today incorporates all information for basic information systems, such as Gopher and WAIS, as well as sophisticated multimedia and hypertext information from many organizations" (Berners-Lee et al. 1993: 1). The Web is also the first entry to introduce "exploitation tools," which allow the user to integrate their own resources with the Internet resources. Thus, using hypertext you could create links from information in your own personal computer to information on the Internet (Krol 1992: 232). There are a number of clients for WWW servers but Mosaic, a hypertext-based user interface, seems to be the lead contender.

As these applications come into general use as a way of mediating the resources on the Internet, several things must be accomplished to make them an effective part of the virtual library tool kit. First, interface design must take human factors into account more seriously. This means coordination of design among system developers, the application of standards within which each of these systems operates, and better use of cognitive psychology research in developing graphical user interfaces. It is still perilously easy for an ordinary user to become lost on the

Internet, leading to frustration and decreasing the likelihood that they will discover something useful. One possible solution is the application of electronic reference documents (ERDs) which "let you use computer power to locate answers to your problems quickly. . . . But ERDs are not a mature technology. For example, consistent end-user features and inter-faces have not appeared. And ERD production practices and techniques still need standardization" (Murray 1993: 121).

An additional problem that needs to be resolved is the provision of a more subject-oriented approach to the Internet. Recently, a subject-based interface design was suggested "involving three search strategies as a front end to the Internet's current format-oriented interface. The three search strategies are: (1) search by specific subject; (2) search from a list of subjects; (3) search for a subject within a format" (Ahrens and Esquer 1993: 1). This approach is intended to overcome two problems of the Internet: First, "users are required to have an unreasonable amount of technical background and knowledge" and, second, "the Internet uses no standard cataloguing or classifying system" (Ahrens and Esquer 1993: 1–2).

It is equally problematic that the basic foundation of indexing in all these systems is word-based with keyword and Boolean logic IR. Some tools like WAIS have introduced the use of weighted relevance measures, but these are a long way from the full use of natural language processing. They have no ability to evaluate context or morphological capability. Krol gives an excellent example in a search for documents that contain "Bush" and "Quayle." The resulting search in WAIS will give a very high value to a document that contains "1000 matches for 'and' but no matches for 'Bush' or 'Quayle'" (Krol 1992: 213). The traditional methods for dealing with this sort of problem, like stopword indexes, will not overcome the basic problem of the lack of full NLP.

Because a long-standing weakness in library system development has been the lack of attention to the question of user interface design and the human factors that underlie it, we must understand the psychology of human information-seeking behaviors, and we must shape the systems through this understanding. It has been demonstrated in studies of under-graduates that their continuing motivation to obtain information when there is no requirement or external pressure to do so "rests on quite different psychological needs. Individuals with a strong need for the approval of others or self-extension, pursue friends, acquaintances and family as information sources. On the other hand, those who have a high need for intellectual stimulation and professional success, as opposed to more human interaction, are inclined to use libraries and experts such as their teachers as information sources" (Dunn 1986: 475, 476, 479). Such varying needs indicate, at least, that we should continue to emphasize making libraries and library systems user-friendly. Basically, this means that system interfaces must incorporate design features that take human factors into account. Since the early 1970s "specialists with backgrounds in applied experimental psychology or industrial engineering have attempted to develop guidelines for system interfaces based on their understanding of basic principles underlying human information processing and cognition and on experimental research" (Normore 1982: 217).

In the larger context of the virtual library, it becomes doubly important to ensure that human factors are taken into account. The original mental picture of library systems is no longer useful as a model for system development. Initially, library systems were designed to automate basic library functions and then to provide access to bibliographic records of items held in the local collection. This view was reflected in the common parlance "OPAC," meaning online public access catalog. OPACs were typically mainframe based with terminal interfaces. The advent of distributed computing should cause a shift in thinking about access to library information. Now, the vision is of client software running on the user's desktop computer and retrieving bibliographic, full-text, and (eventually) multimedia information stored on servers located at various sites. The user interface of the virtual library client must enable users to easily navigate an increasingly complex information environment and manipulate the information retrieved. To this end, focus has shifted to graphical user interfaces with conventions that are native to particular hardware platforms. To understand how we will provide access in the future, we must think in terms of the common user interface, not the OPACs. To crib a slogan, "It's the GUI, stupid."

PROTOTYPES AND PROBLEMS AT CARNEGIE MELLON

We recognize that the Carnegie Mellon computing environment offers unique opportunities to experiment with the application of advanced information technologies and participate in the process of redefining what libraries will be in the technological future. Our approach, since the initiation of the Mercury Project in 1988, has been to assume that others would supply the basic library management system to deal with traditional library functions, and we need not undertake this effort. That is why we have entered into a contract with NOTIS Systems, Inc., to be the alpha test site for the new Horizon system and to transfer several Mercury/LIS technologies to NOTIS. Our resources have been devoted to providing services not readily available from vendors and using advanced IT to do so. When the Mercury Project ended in 1992, the Library Information System was implemented (Troll, *Project Mercury* 1993: 1–16). However, we inherited from Mercury a number of problems and new opportunities to continue significant work. Among the most important was the need to reengineer the LIS interface.

LIS has both a terminal-based and a "point-and-click" Motif interface. This LIS GUI was developed under great pressure of time and has many flaws, which result from lack of attention to human factors. However, user protocols have become a standard feature of GUI client development at the University Libraries, although that has not always been the case. From them, we have learned much of what we know about the shortcomings of our interface design. It is also true that adherence to standards—in this case, the Motif style guide—is now accepted as a central part of our design of user interfaces. The alternative is wasteful—to place greater demands on public services staff to explain how a poorly designed interface works.

The other problem with the LIS GUI is the client architecture, which has remained unchanged since it was implemented in 1991. This architecture, which has been referred to as "spaghetti code," requires a substantial amount of programmer time to achieve the modest goal of maintaining it in production. It is not designed with long-term maintenance and development in mind. Four basic solutions will be used to solve the current problems: (1) differentiate between the user interface code and the common routines it calls to get information for presentation on the workstation; (2) reduce the complexity of the code by eliminating the codependence between software modules; (3) comply with user interface style guidelines, and the results of user protocols; and (4) apply basic standards such as Z39.50 and Z39.58. The purpose of all this work is to establish a highly flexible modular design that allows us to "mix and match, plug and play" new services, particularly Internet-based services like OCLC's FirstSearch or CARL's UnCover and those offered by other library vendors, such as the new NOTIS Horizon library management system, which we are alpha testing.[1]

Among the most advanced technologies of the Mercury/LIS Project has been the development of high-level capacity to distribute bitmapped images across our campus network. We have not yet released access on campus to the image software, but it is available to testers both in the University Libraries and in some departments. The image system allows the user to search periodical indexes in LIS and retrieve full journal images for display. In addition, the user may use the "document browser" to locate a journal title, browse an ASCII table of contents, and display articles from the TOC. This structure mimics online the print journal environment. Surprisingly, the principle obstacle to releasing journal images to the campus has not been the server and retrieval software, but design and functionality of the user interface. To date, several image user interfaces have been built and tested, and the new LIS client will have another.

The prototype implementation of journal images consists of the 43 materials-science journals in Elsevier's three-year TULIP project, of which Carnegie Mellon is one of several participants. The TULIP journals were released for public use in the Spring of 1994. This body of data will grow to no more than 40 gigabytes of information. We have also entered into a three-year joint development project with University Microfilms International called the "Virtual Library Project." UMI's database of journals will present greater challenges from two perspectives—a far larger amount of storage is required and the maintenance of varied storage media. Encompassing over 600 titles, each jukebox alone will have 150 gigabytes, and by the end of the project the total will approach a terabyte of information. Clearly, the LIS image architecture using magnetic storage will become too expensive at $1,000 per gigabyte. The alternative architecture we will develop is a hard-disk-based UNIX cache server of at most 50 gigabytes that will act as a front-end cache for articles that are of recent publication date or high use. CD-ROM jukeboxes will serve as the storage medium for the largest part of the lower use backfiles. The cache server will be integrated into our LIS image system architecture.

I should emphasize that the larger storage capacities required in these projects are dependent on the use of a bitmapped "picture" of the full text—the least efficient format we could choose. This in turn is a function of the retrograde way the full text had to be acquired, that is, by scanning printed journals. Both Elsevier and UMI have made a preliminary effort to overcome this by Optical Character Recognition (OCR) conversion to ASCII. The OCR process is no more than 98 percent effective at best and introduces new problems. Ultimately, we know that these problems are all idiosyncratic and will be addressed as electronic publishing using technologies like Standard Generalized Markup Language (SGML) become widespread.

For both TULIP and the Virtual Library Project, Carnegie Mellon will undertake large-scale monitoring of usage, while ensuring the privacy of individual users. We will be able to test many financial models that relate to issues such as cost recovery and payment of fees. Equally important in the long run, close observation of the full-text journal usage online will give us our first opportunity to really understand how patrons will react to a significant body of literature available in a digital library.

Another primary effort of the Mercury/LIS Project was the presentation of full-text ASCII databases. For several years we have offered online the Academic American Encyclopedia and UMI's Business Dateline, which represents 200 full-text regional business journals and selective text from 100 more. We use OCLC's Newton software to build the databases and articles are retrieved through LIS using typical keyword/Boolean operators. The results of a typical search are what one might expect—low recall and high precision, high recall and low precision, or neither. The reasons for this failing are well-understood and empirically demonstrated in the literature. These two files present excellent targets for the application of the full power of CLARIT natural language processing for IR. We have already used the encyclopedia as a test bed to build a database of over 60 megabytes in about 20 minutes. We have not yet done serious testing to provide empirical comparisons, but we know from the TREC-I and TREC-II evaluations what the results are likely to be. Anecdotal experimentation with the encyclopedia bears them out. In comparison to LIS retrieval from the encyclopedia, CLARIT NLP retrieval results are strikingly better.

The final exemplar application at Carnegie Mellon falls within a traditional area of library activity that has resisted the use of IT—archives. In the fall of 1993, a consortium of Heinz Family Foundations made a grant to University Libraries of slightly over $1 million for a three-year project with the CLARITECH Corporation to develop a fully digitized archive of the papers of the late Senator H. John Heinz III. In addition to the creation of an archive of over 1 million documents, we will preserve the source documents. An electronic archive should meet the goals of preservation and use envisioned by the Commission for Preservation and Access 1991 Report (see Waters 1991). The Heinz Electronic Library Interactive Online System (HELIOS) will mobilize Mercury/LIS and CLARITECH resources in support of the traditional archiving function to respond to a number of critical archival problems. Preservation will be an essential undertaking. The project will address significant problems of archival management and indexing with the OCR conversion to ASCII of scanned text and the use of CLARITECH NLP to provide information retrieval. System design will include the development of three GUIs—a scanning interface for clerical staff; an archival interface for professionals; and a public interface with two views, one for scholars and one for common users. Finally, archives have always required scholars to take the time to schedule visits and travel to distant sites. With HELIOS, remote scholarly access, which provides place and time independence, becomes a practical reality.

CONCLUSION

To a greater or lesser degree, we are all embarked on a journey of discovery. The primary purpose here has been to draw with broad strokes the essential technological conditions that define the possibilities for the new paradigm. Automation has presented wonderful opportunities for improving libraries over the last quarter of a century, and they have been used effectively. The opportunities offered by the new information technology and information retrieval tools are far more exciting, for they give us a constructive chance to reshape our institutions fundamentally to new conditions. If we are successful, we will not have to worry about what libraries will be and what librarians will do in the next century. Let us hope that we will be able to construct a library paradigm that is as robust as the one we inherited from Cutter, Dewey, Poole, Bowker, Winsor, Jewett, and Billings.

NOTE

1. In June 1994 Ameritech Corporation consolidated all of its library system companies into a single entity and announced the cancellation of the Horizon development effort. Carnegie Mellon immediately began looking for a replacement system with all vendors. By September Carnegie Mellon University and SIRSI Corporation, a leading provider of information technology, announced their intention to enter into agreements for future cooperation on several fronts. Carnegie Mellon will license and install the SIRSI Corporation Unicorn Information Management System. SIRSI and Carnegie Mellon will also enter into a technology transfer agreement to work together in several vital areas. These include advanced usability testing for clients by Carnegie Mellon Libraries. In addition, SIRSI will begin implementing technologies for page image display, digital archiving, and natural language information retrieval developed at Carnegie Mellon. Carnegie Mellon will also work with SIRSI to implement authentication and authorization features that will provide necessary security for data and system integrity in open environments.

REFERENCES

Ahrens, Judith, and Gerardo A. Esquer. 1993. "Proposal for a Subject Oriented User Interface to the Internet." *Proceedings of INET '93*: DBA 1–10.

Barry, Dave. 1994. "The '90s, Looking Back at the Interactive Salad Bar." *Newsweek* (January 3): 53–54.

Berners-Lee, T., et al. 1993. "The World-Wide Web Initiative." *Proceedings of INET '93*: DBC 1–5.

Blair, David C., and M. E. Maron. 1985. "An Evaluation of Retrieval Effectiveness for a Full-Text Document Retrieval System." *Communications of the ACM 28* (March): 289–99.

Bodner, Eric, et al. October 1993. *An Internet Billing Server, MS4 Billing Server Prototype Scope Document*. Pittsburgh, Pennsylvania: Carnegie Mellon University, Information Networking Institute.

Byrne, Alex, and Mary Micco. 1988. "Improving OPAC Subject Access: The ADFA Experiment." *College and Research Libraries* 49 (September): 432–41.

Champine, George A. 1991. *MIT Project Athena, a Model for Distributed Campus Computing*. Boston, Massachusetts: Digital Press.

CLARITECH Corporation. December 1993. *Notes on CLARITECH*. Pittsburgh, Pennsylvania: CLARITECH Corporation.

Dillon, Martin, and Patrick Wenzel. 1990. "Retrieval Effectiveness of Enhanced Bibliographic Records." *Library Hi Tech* (no. 3): 43–46.

Dunn, Kathleen. 1986. "Psychological Needs in Undergraduate Information Seeking Behavior." *College and Research Libraries* (September): 475–81.

Hansen, W. J., and C. Haas. 1988. "Reading and Writing with Computers: A Framework for Explaining Differences in Performance." *Communications of the ACM* (September): 1080–89.

Harman, Donna (ed.). 1993. *The First Text REtrieval Conference (TREC-I)*. NIST Special Publication 500-207. Washington, DC: U.S. Government Printing Office.

Harman, Donna (ed.). Forthcoming. *The Second Text REtrieval Conference (TREC-II)*. NIST Special Publication. Washington, DC: U.S. Government Printing Office.

Harrison, Brian R. and Denise A. Troll. 1993. *Proposal to Rewrite the Library Information System (LIS) client*. Pittsburgh, Pennsylvania: Carnegie Mellon University Libraries, Library Automation.

Hersh, William R., et al. 1992. "Indexing Effectiveness of Linguistic and Non-Linguistic Approaches to Automated Indexing." *Medinfo* 92: 1402–08.

Krol, Ed. 1992. *The Whole Internet User's Guide & Catalog*. Sebastopol, California: O'Reilly & Associates, Inc.

Leong, John. 1992. *The Andrew II Project: Functional Requirements*. Pittsburgh, Pennsylvania: Carnegie Mellon University, Computing Services.

Lowry, Charles B. 1993. "Managing Technology: Perspectives and Prospects for a New Paradigm." *Journal of Academic Librarianship* 19 (September): 237–38, 246.

McKinin, Emma Jean, et al. 1991. "The Medline/Full-Text Research Project." *Journal of the American Society for Information Science* 42 (May): 297–307.

MacKinnon, Sylvia Carson, et al. 1993. "Z39.50 and LIAS: Penn State's Experience." *Information Technology and Libraries* 12 (June): 230–37.

Martin, James. 1981. *Computer Networks and Distributed Processing: Software, Techniques, Architecture*. Englewood Cliffs, New Jersey: Prentice-Hall, Inc.

Morris, James et al. 1986. "Andrew: A Distributed Personal Computing Environment." *Communications of the ACM* 29 (March): 184–201.

Murray, Philip C. 1993. "Documentation Goes Digital." *Byte* (September): 121–29.

Nielsen, Brian, and Betsy Baker. 1987. "Educating the Online Catalog User: A Model Evaluation Study." *Library Trends* (Spring): 571–85.

Normore, L. F. 1982. "Human Factors Considerations in Designing Information Retrieval Systems Interfaces: Some Techniques for Lessening User Effort." *Proceedings of the ASIS Annual Meeting* 19: 217–19.

Pritchard-Schoch, Teresa. 1993. "Natural Language Comes of Age." *Online* (May): 33–43.

Quint, Barbara. 1993. "Easy Does It." *Wilson Library Bulletin* (June): 86–91.

RMG Consultants, Inc. "OSI, Z39.50, and Library Automation." *Papers on Library Automation* (December).

Salton, Gerard. 1989. *Automatic Text Processing: The Transformation, Analysis, and Retrieval of Information by Computer.* Reading, Massachusetts: Addison-Wesley Publishing Company.

Smith, Elizabeth S. 1993. "On the Shoulders of Giants: From Boole to Shannon to Taube: The Origins and Development of Computerized Information from the Mid-19th Century to the Present." *Information Technology and Libraries* 12 (June): 217–26.

Stovel, Lennie, et al. 1993. "RLG's Z39.50 Server: Development and Implementation Issues." *Information Technology and Libraries* 12 (June): 227–30.

Tenopir, Carol. 1993. "Natural Language Searching with WIN." *Library Journal* (November 1): 55–56.

Troll, Denise A. September 1993. *Z39.58 Search Syntax, a Report.* Pittsburgh, Pennsylvania: Carnegie Mellon University, University Libraries.

Troll, Denise A. 1993. *Project Mercury & the Development of the Library Information System.* Mercury Technical Report Series, Number 7. Pittsburgh, Pennsylvania: Carnegie Mellon University.

Van Orden, Richard. 1990. "Content-Enriched Access to Electronic Information: Summaries of Selected Research." *Library Hi Tech* (no. 3): 27–32.

Waters, Donald J. 1991. F*rom Microfilm to Digital Imagery, a Report of the Yale University Library to the Commission on Preservation and Access.* Washington, DC: Commission on Preservation and Access, Association of Research Libraries.

White, Herbert. 1993. "Scholarly Publication, Academic Libraries, and the Assumption That These Processes are Really under Management Control." *College and Research Libraries* (July): 293–301.

7 Impact on the Library School Curriculum and Methods of Teaching

Thomas D. Walker

It has been said that the old and somewhat cloying library is a thing of the past. Some of these musty print collections may be out of date, but they will continue to exist for decades. "Old" and "cloying" can also be applied to some electronic sources. If we consider the latter term in the sense of causing aversion or outright disgust through excess, then "cloying" can be said to refer to a classic case of information overload—a situation encountered during many users' initial exposure to electronic sources. Research is a cumulative activity and library and information science is a cumulative discipline. We should not abandon the past (nor attempt to live in it) but complement it with new methods and technologies. We should do this at a rate fast enough to lead librarians, other researchers, and the general public in the use of emerging technologies.

It is beneficial to approach a seemingly straightforward subject such as the impact of technologies on reference services and bibliographic instruction from multiple perspectives. It is easy for librarians and other information professionals to ignore the role of library education; unfortunately, the reverse occurs as well. In examining the impact of technologies on either practice or education/research, a common assumption is that the flow is one way, that librarians and library educators/researchers have no impact on the development or use of technology. It can be argued that precisely because of the requirements of librarians and library users and because of the research and teaching of library educators, that technologies have spread as fast as they have. This chapter, which is a response to the preceding chapters, addresses the relationship between technologies and library education. Issues of concern include (1) conceptions of technology, (2) the changing functions of technologies in libraries and similar environments, (3) achieving professional competencies for librarians and other information professionals, and (4) the place of library education and research in this period of rapid technological innovation.

CONCEPTIONS OF TECHNOLOGY

Yesterday's technologies are today's traditions. As recently as the eighteenth century, card catalogs were considered novel and were met with bemusement because they were thought not to be as efficient as printed library catalogs and not to be as safe as printed catalogs because their cards or slips might fall out too easily (Blumenschein 1781: vol. 4, 411–412). One librarian simply used the device for alphabetizing entries (Kayser 1790: 39–42). Card catalogs were also embraced on a national scale in France in the late eighteenth century (Smalley 1991: 3–4). It is difficult for us to see the institution of the card catalog as a technology, or as some might define it, as an applied science. Yet it is an example of the science of the application of knowledge to a practical situation, another version of the same definition of technology.

For library education, the impact of technical training and technology were closely intertwined. White (1976: 139–152) enumerated ten educational norms in existence after World War I. The first two are illustrative of the pragmatic approach commonly found at the time:

1. The object is to train students to do effectively the work which the calling requires (White 1976: 139).
2. Professional learning is practical, not theoretical, and as such is separate and distinct from the aims, methods, and results of academic scholarship (White 1976: 139).

Some educators and perhaps a smaller percentage of librarians today would disagree with the positions expressed in the ten guidelines, which did, however, emphasize the practical and changing technologies of the day. It is generally understood that the earliest decades of library education in the United States until the 1920s were an era of technical education (White 1961: 90).

For some early library educators, a distinction was made between "subprofessional duties" and a higher form of technical education (Reese 1936). The presence of handwriting instruction can be documented at the Albany School (New York State Library School) between 1884 and 1903, when typewriting was added (White 1976: 66). In the years leading to the Williamson report (based on a study of library education for the Carnegie Corporation in 1920 and 1921 by Charles C. Williamson, a librarian and statistician), there was a shift from "training in the technique, and even the mechanics, of library work" to an approach that recognized both the clerical and professional aspects of librarianship (Williamson 1923: 32). In the same report, Williamson decries the continued presence of typewriting instruction in professional library education (1923: 32–33).

All this is outside the bounds of the developments of the 1930s at the Graduate Library School of the University of Chicago, which proposed a scholarly approach to the discipline, leaving to other schools the responsibility of training practitioners (Waples 1931: 26–36; White 1976: 233–237). The research-based approach to a developing library science was certainly not universally accepted (Thompson 1931: 743–746; White 1976: 233–237), but that model strongly influenced subsequent philosophies of library education. Training, especially technical training, was to be substantially de-emphasized during the next half century. The acknowledgment of the existence of this academic/technical dichotomy is reflected in the trend, dating back to the 1930s, of the propagation of library schools in academic institutions where attention could be given to academic treatments rather than in libraries (White 1976: 237).

Library educators of today are also concerned about the presence of mechanical training at the graduate level. How much technical ability should our programs assume of incoming students? Entering the twenty-first century, we should take for granted skills such as typing, word processing, and a basic knowledge of computers; for those without such knowledge or abilities, we should provide perhaps some training software or occasional workshops, but no formal training for academic credit. To paraphrase Williamson (1923: 33), why should such skills be required as part of the professional librarian's equipment any more than of the lawyer, accountant, journalist, teacher, or any other professional?

However, a negative perception of training versus education has so permeated professional library education, that some relevant, intellectually sophisticated, profession-specific technical skills are unnecessarily downplayed. The popular and professional conceptions of technology have changed.

THE CHANGING FUNCTIONS OF TECHNOLOGY

During the last 75 years, the spectrum of technologies has widened and deepened. The differences between advanced clerical technologies and elementary professional technologies are not always clear. Delmus Williams, in a previous chapter, was correct in suggesting that for many years technological changes occurred slowly enough to accommodate those librarians who were reluctant to change. With so many and such varied technological advances, it is necessary for librarians to be technologically literate from the start of their careers and to keep abreast of future changes. For library educators, the challenge is to provide practical and theoretical foundations for the careers of every student.

The goal is not merely to provide training in a few current technical areas. Recent electronic media have been very ephemeral. Punch cards can now be read by very few machines. It is extremely difficult to find computers capable of reading CP-M operating system disks. How long will the current technologies exist? Change can occur when one technology evolves into or is replaced by another and also—and librarians should be keenly aware of this possibility—when media exist side-by-side and grow in a cumulative way. The book and other print media will be here for centuries; although it may be possible to store the contents of a research library in a book-sized object, it does not necessarily follow that print will soon be replaced. Technological obsolescence threatens library and information science just as severely as it does other professions and disciplines with important technological components. To convey a sense of the evolving nature of technologies is one of the many objectives of library education.

ACHIEVING PROFESSIONAL COMPETENCIES

In his chapter, George Machovec mentions the existence of incoherent piles of "unrelated building blocks" in libraries. Similar piles of blocks may be found in schools of library and information science. Technologies have influenced the daily activities of library school staff, faculty, and students and have acquired a prominent place in graduate curricula. A recent study of networking education in schools of library and information science in the United States and Canada demonstrates that almost all such programs value networking skills (Wittig and Wolfram 1994). Further, the study shows that most schools believe that some technical knowledge and skills, in this case those concerned with the Internet, should be found throughout the curriculum, not ideally in separate courses. This might be one way to avoid one more isolated "building block" in programs of library education.

Technologies have affected instruction in many ways. Although some of the traditional media, such as overhead projectors, slides, films, and videos, will continue to see use for a long time, they have been joined by electronic technologies that have emerged during the last few years. Computers have been used in library education for more than two decades. They are seeing more and more use in and out of the classroom, and auxiliary equipment that allows for classroom display has become frequently used. Liquid crystal diode (LCD) panels, for use with overhead projectors, large-screen monitors for classroom use, and specially networked computer labs have been established for interactive instruction.

The demographics of higher education, including library education, have shifted to older and less centralized student populations. For this reason, distance education has been increasingly used, with technologies playing a role. Static videos, one-way transmissions, multidirectional radio/video connections (audiographics, videographics), and compressed video have all seen useful applications. Internet instruction is not only a possibility, but has taken place and will become more important in the near future.

Categories of Technical Knowledge

As implied by Machovec, it is clear that a knowledge of individual products or specialized searching techniques is not sufficient to prepare librarians for the future. They must also be conversant with issues at more general levels: systems, systems design, interfaces, information policy, the CD-ROM industry, management issues, licensing arrangements, and more. At the same time, it is vital that librarians possess a thorough knowledge of traditional print sources that will continue to be the backbone of research in many fields for decades to come.

The following suggestions, some of which were inspired by Johannah Sherrer's chapter, are a preliminary list of competencies for librarians. Included are areas with some technological components; not included are fundamental areas such as library history, intellectual freedom, philosophies of library service, and preservation.

Professional Competencies

Research abilities
    General acquaintance with systems of organizing knowledge
    General knowledge of research methods in a variety of disciplines
    Knowledge of a variety of library types and extra-library sources
    Knowledge of information sources in print and electronic formats

Ability to use finding aids in print and electronic formats, including network
    tools, such as Gopher, World-Wide Web, and Mosaic
Reference abilities
    Knowledge of reference request types
        Bibliographic assistance
        Fact finding
        Directional
        Research
        Document delivery
        Technical assistance
    Ability to match requests to sources and methods, regardless of format
Teaching abilities
    Bibliographic instruction
Technical services abilities
    Collection development
    Acquisitions
    Processing
    Cataloging
        Copy cataloging
        Original cataloging
        Catalog maintenance
Technical support abilities
    Consortium level
    Library system level
    Library level
    Library automation
    Mainframe
    LAN (choice, setup, applications, support)
    CD-ROM (setup and support)
    PC (choice, setup, and support)

Unexplored thus far have been technical competencies in schools of
library and information science. It should be assumed that faculty collectively possess the knowledge and abilities found among information
professionals. Faculty, staff, and students alike experience technological
advances in the course of their respective activities. The following are
some of the areas of competence encountered now or in the near future by
these groups:

Administrative
    Knowledge of networks (local and wide area), PCs, and mainframes
    Knowledge of commonly available software such as word processors, spread-
        sheets, databases, statistical software, and scheduling programs

Technical
  Knowledge of networks (local and wide area), PCs, and mainframes
  Knowledge of commonly available software such as word processors, spread-
    sheets, databases, statistical software, and scheduling programs
  Knowledge of instructional technologies
Instruction/Research
  Knowledge of networks (local and wide area), PCs, and mainframes
  Knowledge of commonly available software such as word processors, spread-
    sheets, databases, statistical software, and additional software depending on
    specialties
  Knowledge of instructional technologies
  Ability to search online and CD-ROM databases

The Wittig and Wolfram study (1994) indicates that most schools surveyed (71 percent) believed that it was important to present practical training in conjunction with related theoretical topics. Sherrer states that "database commands are increasingly transparent, whereas the definition and composition of databases are often masked." Although this may make it ever easier for end-users, it implies that the importance of database structures and functions have to be conveyed to professional users at some point. What is a database? What can a database do? What is the purpose of a given database? What is it scope? Which database, if any, is appropriate for a given question? How can one evaluate electronic sources? These are all kinds of questions that can be addressed in formal education programs. By confronting problems such as these in formal settings, students should be able to respond to related situations in the future.

Charles Lowry likewise illustrates some of the reasons to support practical training with a theoretical foundation. Difficulties encountered during full-text searching, such as low precision caused by linguistic problems, can be illuminated by formal study of recall/precision ratios, indexing practices, Boolean retrieval, and more.

Should we focus exclusively on user needs and use all technologies available to us on a daily basis as Sherrer suggests? In an ideal setting, yes. Realistically, however, each situation has to be evaluated with cost in mind. Which is more cost effective, maintaining an expensive standing order for a specialized but seldom-used statistical source or phoning directly to the source or carrying out an online search on a need basis? Although libraries must regard new and emerging technologies as fundamental to everyday services, judgment is still part of the equation and part of the reason to go beyond mere technical training in library schools.

John Tyson, in his chapter on the impact of technologies on library clientele, summarizes some areas of concern for library users. All three apply equally well to future library professionals who must (1) understand the structures of information, (2) understand technological advances, and (3) be able to evaluate sources of information. Tyson is also correct in his recommendation regarding access to new technologies by citizens who have no such access at home or work. Libraries have long been resource-shaping institutions and, in the case of emerging technologies, this situation is complicated by widely varying levels of information literacy. Library education programs have to provide opportunities for students to learn how to anticipate and meet the information and educational needs of users.

Tyson, however, makes several assumptions early in his chapter:

A necessary first step would be to ensure that all information specialists working in libraries receive training to serve as intermediaries in connecting library clients to local, statewide, and global electronic networks and in guiding users to appropriate information resources via these networks. Once the library workforce is trained, it will be incumbent on the library profession to assist in educating and training the citizenry at large.

There is nothing to argue with here; however, the enormity of the training problems may have been underestimated. Being primarily concerned with education, library educators work hard to accomplish Tyson's first step, which is a very big one, for a very small group: new librarians. Ensuring that all information specialists receive training is a gigantic task. Technologies obsolesce. The Telnets, FTPs, and Gophers we teach today are being superseded at this moment. Access to technology varies tremendously. Even if we could reach the thousands of information professionals tomorrow, only a limited number would be able to, for instance, start applying their knowledge of the Internet within a few months. Should we travel and train? Should we teach the Internet over the Internet as is currently being done at the University of Illinois? Should we train trainers? All of these issues, and perhaps more, have to be addressed before we will be able to say "once the library workforce is trained." Training researchers and the general public is important, as Tyson suggests, and it is incumbent on all of us to educate and train them as we do the same for ourselves. A method that has been very successful at the School of Library and Information Science of the University of Wisconsin-Milwaukee results in benefits for practicing librarians, library users, and library students. By establishing internships, teaching assistantships, and field work courses with significant instructional components—often with emphases on the

Internet, CD-ROM products, or other electronic sources or media—the program provides training for librarians and library users and teaching experience for students.

Library and Information Science Courses with an Emphasis on Technology

Although slightly more than half of library school educators felt that networking sources should be introduced throughout the curriculum (Wittig and Wolfram 1994), other technologies have long been included. Certain courses, however, have been concerned with technical topics for a long time, some for decades. The following is a representative selection of course types from the course catalogs of six schools of library and information science in the Midwest and on both coasts. Of course, there are more that could be added, especially those in large, interdisciplinary units. It should be clear from this short list alone that technologies have had an important impact on library education.

- *Educational media*: With or without connections to a department or school of education, these courses, which aim to introduce students to traditional and emerging educational technologies, have a long tradition.
- *Bibliographic control of library materials*: This kind of course is perhaps the oldest among library school courses with technical components, including the study and creation of MARC, searching of OCLC and other bibliographic utilities, and the use of appropriate bibliographic CD-ROMs.
- *Library automation*: By its very nature a technical course that can focus on databases and the analysis and design of automated systems.
- *Research methods*: A regular offering of larger schools and those with doctoral programs, these courses have concentrated on methods in the social sciences, especially statistical methodologies, some of which require exposure to statistical software.
- *Reference courses*: A special challenge for these courses has involved retaining sufficient coverage of traditional sources, while attempting to cover existing and emerging technologies, including the use of online public-access catalogs, CD-ROM sources and indexes, specially designed local databases, and the Internet.
- *Legal bibliography/librarianship*: Coverage of WESTLAW and LEXIS, not to mention traditional print sources, has been augmented by applications of Internet sources and records management systems.
- *Business bibliography/librarianship/competitive intelligence*: Another specialized course with attention given to online sources, an ever-increasing

variety of CD-ROM products, electronic communication, and Internet sources exemplify the range of technological advances that can serve as a model for other specialized courses.

- *Computer courses*: Although some librarians have had extensive experience with computers (or have acquired computer science degrees) before entering library school, the first significant contact with computers for many librarians occurs in library schools. The range of courses is especially wide in the large interdisciplinary library and information science programs. Most schools offer the students an option of taking courses in computer science departments. Following is a list of some of the courses offered in library schools: Introduction to computers, Programming languages, Database design and evaluation, Database software evaluation, Library automation, and Online searching.

- *Workshops*: Intended either for students or practicing librarians, sometimes for credit, workshops provide concentrated practical training, often for topics that are not best covered in courses. Workshops or other training sessions offered in library schools, libraries, and by commercial organizations concentrate on CD-ROM products, OPACs, Database software (dBASE IV, InMagic, Fox-Pro), Internet, and Online training (LEXIS, NEXIS, DIALOG, citation indexes, business indexes).

THE PLACE OF LIBRARY EDUCATION AND RESEARCH IN A PERIOD OF RAPID TECHNOLOGICAL INNOVATION

If there is any one goal of library education and research today, it may be to contribute to an understanding of the nature of knowledge. People have been fascinated by this topic for millennia; we happen to live in a time of technological innovation that allows us to conceive of information in ways we never have before. By considering library and information science to be a kind of meta-science—one that touches all disciplines and institutions, yet is independent of them; one that takes advantage of relevant methods from other fields, yet develops some of its own; and one that confronts certain matters of information, which while of concern to all disciplines and institutions, are not regarded to be within their individual realms—we can ensure it a prominent place in society.

Johannah Sherrer suggests that librarians look to other institutions for inspiration. This may be an especially useful approach to learn about acquisitions practices, inventory control, and other technical activities in environments driven by a need to be fast and profitable. Libraries can be more efficient. Perhaps by being aware of technical advances found in other fields or institutions, we can adapt them for our own specialized situations. Parenthetically, there are some possible additions to the time-table of information handling, for which Sherrer has invited contributions: the field of epistemology; the field of bibliography and its many major figures, such as Konrad Gesner (1545) and Theodore Besterman (1965); landmarks in the history of encyclopedias, including the famous Diderot/d'Alembert Encyclopédie (1957–1780), which was the ency-clopedia of the Enlightenment and was based on a classification of knowledge, which was based in turn on a scheme of Francis Bacon, with roots back to Aristotle; and major classificationists, such as Ranganathan (1965).

Models of Knowledge

Different metaphors have been used to describe the nature of recorded knowledge. In his chapter about bibliographic instruction, Sager suggested moving from a model of the earth with clearly delineated national bounda-ries, which represents the traditional print culture, to an electronic world view in which the globe is seen from such a distance that the boundaries are blurred—a perspective that promotes a holistic understanding of the knowledge realm. Such an image is powerful in its simplicity.

An alternative and more abstract conceptual model, which integrates all media and changes over time, is less concrete and perhaps less memorable than the Sager electronic worldview, but can offer a more complex solution than a sphere: an amorphous blob model, which can be thought of as a four-dimensional execution of two-dimensional bibliometric mapping. Some bibliometricians have proposed planar maps consisting of one or several groups of related areas of research. Considering the vast literature represented in the three citation indexes of the Institute for Scientific Information, not to mention the even more overwhelming literature out-side of that system, one can imagine the advantage of conceiving of these knowledge maps in three dimensions. Representing the state of knowledge over time, these amorphous blobs take on a fourth dimension. Following are some characteristics of this model:

- *Size of blobs*: The larger the area of research the larger the blob.
- *Shape of blobs and the nature of recorded knowledge*: This three-dimensional model allows for the inclusion of popular treatments of subjects, syntheses intended for specialists, educational works, as well as cutting-edge research. The more general an approach, the closer to the center of a blob it would be located—a location not likely to increase the size of the blob or to change the shape of the blob. A groundbreaking study would be represented at the surface

of the blob, expanding its volume to a degree related to its contribution to knowledge and perhaps changing the shape of the blob in some way.

- *Relative disciplinarity of research*: Some fields are quite self-contained, some relate closely to similar areas of research, and others are interdisciplinary. For this model, the more interdisciplinary a field of research, the more porous the blob's membrane. An isolated area of research would have an impenetrable membrane; if the area becomes less isolated, the membrane would become porous to an appropriate degree.

- R*elative pace of research*: For different areas of research, advances in scholarship and technology are made at different speeds. The quicker the movement of an area of research, the more liquid its blob. A fast field would be represented by a thin liquid; a relatively static area of research would have a relatively thick consistency; a field in which knowledge did not increase or change at all would be solid.

What is the best model of recorded knowledge for educating library and other information professionals? A virtual library is a possibility, yet as experienced researchers know, the world has been a virtual library all along. An electronic worldview as proposed by Sager may be useful because its beauty and simplicity are so striking. A seething primordial soup of amorphous blobs may be closer to the true nature of knowledge. Perhaps there is no single model of knowledge that is best. Epistemologists have been concerned with the nature of knowledge for a long time, as will we be. New technologies have forced us to think about the nature of knowledge and recorded knowledge in new ways. Perhaps the best models for library educators are those that will help students of various academic backgrounds and different levels of maturity confront the nature of knowledge in whatever media it may be represented.

Library Education as Gesamtkunstwerk

A very appropriate model for library education curriculum design can be adapted from Richard Wagner's idea of Gesamtkunstwerk, an approach to opera that integrated musical and non-musical elements: music, dance, poetry, architecture, sculpture, painting, drama, art, literature, religion, mythology, and costume (Wagner 1850). It is not simply a combination of all these various things, but a fusion into an integrated whole. Although not of Wagnerian proportions—we have no legendary figures except perhaps for Callimachus and St. Jerome—library education should also be an interprise that combines elements from all existing and emerging media. Library and information science students come from a very wide variety of backgrounds, and it may be through certain leitmotiv that thread their ways throughout the curriculum, that the students are brought together and that the many and various issues, topics, methods, strategies, and resources are unified into a whole. In other words, the whole of a library education curriculum is greater than the sum of its individual parts because it brings them all together in a useful, integrated way.

A Wagnerian approach to the organization of knowledge and library education may help to provide a concrete structure useful in integrating the many disciplines related to our own. Library and information science educational programs, unlike Wagner's music-dramas, should have an element of planned redundancy. By introducing aspects of technology, such as electronic information retrieval, in more than one place in the curriculum, it is possible to reinforce understanding of topics. By having some built-in redundancy, aspects of traditional bibliography and technology would be both isolated and integrated.

A Symbiosis between Libraries and Library Education

With the ever-increasing and ever-quickening layering of traditional and emerging technologies, library education (by whatever name), will assume a more prominent and visible role. Indeed, it will be necessary to adopt a symbiotic relationship between libraries and library education that will allow both to keep abreast of technological advances. It should be a relationship in which both institutions are dependent on one another, receive reinforcement from one another, and are in every way mutually beneficial.

There is no question that technology has influenced and will continue to affect programs of library education. From announcements for such positions as reference/technology librarians to more specialized "Internet Librarians" and an e-text cataloger for a center for electronic texts, it is possible to see how important it is to prepare beginning professionals with technical knowledge and skills. Likewise, for practicing librarians, technologies have created a growing demand for continuing education in the form of extracurricular courses and workshops.

REFERENCES

Besterman, Theodore. 1965. *World Bibliography of Bibliographies*. 4th ed. Lausanne: Societas Bibliographica.

Blumenschein, Adalbert. ca. 1765–1781. "Beschreibung verschiedener Bibliotheken in Europa." Manuscript, sterreiche Nationalbibliothek (Vienna), Handschriftensammlung MS Ser. nov. 2807-2810.

Diderot, Denis, and Jean Le Rond d'Alembert. 1757–1780. *Encyclopédie, ou Diction-naire raisonné des sciences, des arts et des métiers.* 35 vols. Paris: David, Briasson, LeBreton, and Durand.

Gesner, Konard. 1545. *Bibliotheca universalis.* Zurich.

Kayser, Albrecht Christoph. 1790. *Iber die Manipulation bey der Einrichtung einer Bibliothek und der Verfertigung der Bⁿcherverzeichnisse....* Bayreuth: Verlag der Zeitungsdruckerei.

Ranganathan, S. R. 1965. *The Colon Classification.* New Brunswick, N.J.: Rutgers University, Graduate School of Library Service.

Reece, Ernest J. 1936. *The Curriculum in Library Schools.* New York: Columbia University Press.

Smalley, Joseph. 1991. "The French Cataloging Code of 1791: A Translation." *Library Quarterly* 61: 1–14.

Thompson, D. Seymour. 1931. "Do We Want a Library Science?" *Library Journal* 56: 743–746.

Wagner, Richard. 1850. Das Kunstwerk der Zukunft. In *Sämtliche Schriften und Dichtun-gen.* 6th ed. Vol. 3. Leipzig: Breitkopf & Härtel, (1914): 42–177.

Waples, Douglas. 1931. "The Graduate Library School, University of Chicago." *Library Quarterly* 1: 26–36.

White, Carl M. 1976. *A Historical Introduction to Library Education: Problems and Progress to 1951.* Metuchen, N.J.: Scarecrow.

White, Carl M. 1961. *The Origins of the American Library School.* Metuchen, N.J.: Scarecrow.

Williamson, Charles C. 1923. *Training for Library Service.* Boston: Merrymount Press. Also published in *The Williamson Reports of 1921 and 1923.* Metuchen, N.J.: Scarecrow (1971).

Wittig, Constance, and Wolfram, Dietmar. 1994. "A Survey of Networking Education in North American Library Schools." *Library Trends* 42 (Spring 1994): 626–637.

8 Information Transfer, Information Technology, and the New Information Professional

Herbert K. Achleitner

Economics and technology are the engines of modern society and play a dominant role in shaping the future. Information technology, because computerized telecommunication works so well, is defining the role of information professionals. The critical question for information professionals is: How does information technology change our organization and our role as information professionals? Can we successfully shift from warehousing books to digitized information service? What belief system, values, knowledge base, and tools will help us navigate in this turbulent sea? Which answers we choose, which pathways we travel, which companions we select, will influence our success in the journey into the future.

As we enter the digitized world, the necessity of transforming our vision, goals, and values intensifies. Transformation implies change in the way we perceive reality, think, do our job, love, and prepare for a successful career. In past history, radical shifts meant a struggle between the forces of change and continuity; now change is viewed as an opportunity, a mission, a chance for creativity. Some consider this shift as great as any in the history of human civilization, and label it a "paradigm shift" (Drucker 1993).

TOWARD AN INFORMATION SOCIETY

We may recall that agrarian societies with low productivity and limited control over their environment were transformed in a relatively short time into societies with high technological capabilities. A firm belief in the unhampered ability to achieve progress and betterment of the human condition emerged. For the first time, we gained control over the environment and developed the ability to convert natural resources into a steady stream of products. Mechanization shaped the lifestyle of the working class, fostered urbanization, and stratified the political landscape through emergence of the working-class-oriented political parties.

The evolution of the industrial paradigm had a revolutionary impact on work patterns. Workers migrated from farms to cities and the proportion of agricultural workers declined sharply. With mechanization, productivity increased, the cost of farm products declined, and an ever smaller number of people were needed in agriculture. Interestingly enough, a similar process took place in advanced industrial countries. After several hundred years of industrial expansion, continued growth of industries stopped and even declined as industrialization migrated to less developed countries. Ironically, in place of mechanization, computer-assisted automation started to create unemployment. Job creation did not keep up with the speed at which automation made jobs obsolete. The merging of computers and telecommunications is shifting the economy to a situation where information-related activities play a critical role in opening the world marketplace. The result is a massive restructuring in virtually every segment of society. This transition from the industrial world and the restructuring of economies has brought forth the terms "postindustrial" economy, "service" economy, or "information" economy.

In industrialized countries, the shift toward an information-based economy means, among other things, that a majority of the workforce is employed in information-related businesses. Moreover, more and more industrialized countries are following the path toward becoming an information-based society. The pattern is clear: each shift produces opportunities and creates crises; the process is dynamic and ongoing and the implications for individuals and organizations are challenging.

The advent of the information economy did not bring about the end of the agrarian or industrial economies. Rather, all three coexist rather nicely in a complex and interactive system. However, complexity demands new models and a larger framework and new worldviews. A conceptual shift takes place when a new all-encompassing framework is adopted; one where the industrial societies no longer use agrarian models and when information-based societies no longer use mechanistic models (Davis 1987: 194).

ROOTS OF CHANGE

Most of us are aware of the profound changes occurring all around us. The collapse of the Soviet Union and the emergence of a multipolar world, the possibility of peace in the Middle East, the emergence of trading blocks such as the North American Free Trade Agreement (NAFTA), the Southern Cone Group (Argentina, Brazil, Paraguay, and Uruguay) and expansion of the European Community are just some examples of fundamental reorganizations taking place.

The fundamental restructuring of such large and dominant corporations like IBM and AT&T is another example showing that change affects even the most powerful corporations. This is exemplified by a massive layoff of workers and the formation of strategic alliances among competitors, for example, IBM and Apple Computers. What we are witnessing is a response to an open, dynamic, competitive marketplace. Wherever one looks, whether to countries, organizations, or individuals, they are changing the way they view the world, think, work, or do business. It is a kind of deep change that a paradigm shift implies. But what are the causes of this change and what are the roots?

In his enormously influential book, Thomas Kunn (1970) describes the concept of paradigm to mean the fundamental assumptions about the nature of the world. Scientists, like most of us, go about their daily tasks within a particular framework of assumptions about what are legitimate problems, what are the solutions, and what methods can be used to understand them. A paradigm is shared assumptions and practices held by a scientific community. In effect, paradigms go beyond the scientific and have relevance for society as a whole.

Kuhn introduces the concept of "stages" that lead toward a scientific revolution. The first stage is the preparadigm stage where several schools of thought compete. Competition is fierce, no real rules exist. Normal science constitutes the second stage: a time of problem solving and a time when a discipline accepts the most popular paradigm. The next stage is the anomaly stage in which problems keep reoccurring and cannot be solved under the rules of the old paradigm. This leads to the crisis stage in which the focus is on anomalies, which become the focus of research. Extraordinary science is the last stage and is similar to the preparadigm stage. Normal rules of science are relaxed and schools of thought begin to develop.

During a paradigm shift, the new paradigm emerges in outline form. This is a period when not only competing schools of thought thrive, but also a time when different worldviews and different value systems operate simultaneously. Rather than stability and predictability, chaos, discontinuity, and change are the norm. These are the circumstances under which we find ourselves today. We have inherited the rules and techniques of yesterday, yet information technology has pushed people and organizations into a crisis stage. The old rules are no longer valid, and new rules have yet to emerge. What Kuhn tells us is that this is normal in a time of crises and revolutionary change, that new rules are here, and we have to unlearn and relearn.

EMERGENT PARADIGM

In a remarkable work, Peter Schwartz and James Ogilvy (1979), formerly of the Stanford Research Institute, analyzed the emergence of the new paradigm by studying a number of disciplines and disciplinelike areas. They reviewed disciplines such as physics, chemistry, mathematics, philosophy, politics, psychology, linguistics, and religion as well as disciplinelike areas such as brain theory, ecology, evolution, and consciousness. From this analysis they identify seven characteristic shifts between the dominant and emergent paradigms. Achleitner and Hale (1988) analyzed these characteristics and prepared Table 8.1 as a summary of their findings.

Paradigms involve concepts, values, perceptions, and practices that are tacitly agreed on by a community. Thus, for example, the old paradigm stands for a patriarchal order with an obsession for order, domination, and control whether in science, technology, or society. It holds a mechanistic worldview where the material universe is pictured as a mechanical system and the human body is viewed as a machine. Linear thinking is dominant and underlies our thinking about material processes.

In the emergent paradigm, however, relationships are weblike and intrinsically dynamic. Reality is perceived as a network of relationships where hierarchies disappear. Scientific theories and models cannot provide complete understanding, and truth is not what science is about. Finally, reality can only be described to a limited extent.

People, society, science, technology, and organizations are adapting to the emergent worldview. It is the thesis of this chapter that if we understand the intellectual revolution taking place in many disciplines then we have signposts for the future. Mutual causality tells us that we cannot predict the future, but we can analyze dominant trends that give us a glimpse of the future. Taking the view that organizations function best in an open system, where diversity is encouraged, complexity is viewed positively, and mutual causality is a dynamic process of change

Table 8.1
Dominant/Emergent Paradigm and Associated Beliefs

Dominant/Emergent Paradigms	*Associated Beliefs*
From simple toward complex views of phenomena being investigated	Diversity, interaction, and open systems are symptoms of the emerging reality. An entity cannot be separated from its interactive environment. Complex systems develop "unique properties" and a system can no longer be perceived as the "sum of its parts."
From hierarchic toward heterarchic views of order inherent in the world being studied	The old notion of order was based on the concept of hierarchy. God was seen as the Prime Mover. The emergent concept is that there may be no natural order, that orders exist side by side.
From mechanical toward holographic metaphors used to describe the phenomena being studied	The machine (Newtonian mechanics) metaphor is replaced by the hologram. Images in the hologram are created through a dynamic process of interaction. Information is distributed throughout the image. Pieces of the whole are evident throughout the system.
From a view that the unknown can be determined toward an acceptance that the future is indeterminate	Heisenberg's Indeterminacy Principle states that at a subatomic level the future state of a particle is in principle not predictable. In complex systems the future cannot be predicted.
From linear toward a mutual view of causality	Distinction between cause and effect is meaningless. The new paradigm adds positive feedback and feedforward.
From a view of change as a planned assembly of events toward change morphogenetically	A system that functions under conditions of openness, diversity, complexity, mutual causality, and indeterminacy changes morphogenetically. Change occurs unpredictably.
From objective research toward perspective research	Perception, instruments, and disciplines are not neutral.

and continuity, means we have to become more opportunistic, flexible, and innovative. Information technology is the tool that fosters the motivation.

INFORMATION TECHNOLOGIES
AND ORGANIZATIONS

A brief sample of recent publications by Drucker (1989, 1993); Michael Ray and Alan Rinzler (1993); Don Tapscott and Art Caston

(1993); Stephen Bradley, Jerry Hausman, Richard Nolan (1993); and Linda Harasim (1994) describe the enormous impact information technologies are having on virtually every aspect and function in an organization. Examples include relations with customers, shifting partnerships with suppliers and competitors, forced restructuring of national economies and individual businesses, and ongoing globalization of the marketplace. In librarianship a similar revolution is manifesting itself. In the preceeding chapters on the impact of emerging technologies, the authors discuss in great detail the emerging information technology infrastructure and the opportunities they afford us. The merging of computers and telecommunications makes this dynamic change possible and, in effect, inevitable.

The trend in the 1990s is toward networked information systems, information management systems functioning in real time, retrieval of information for rapid decision making, and systems that are nonlinear and have multimedia capabilities. As Don Tapscott and Art Caston observed (1993: 7), the enabling effect of information technology not only allows for restructuring, but creates new models for doing things.

THE NEW INFORMATION ENVIRONMENT
AND INFORMATION PROFESSIONALS

Information is both an economic resource and a commodity. The production, dissemination, organization, storage, and use of information has been part of developed society since the advent of printing. However, these processes have gone through a tremendous evolution in the last 20 years as a result of electronic-based information products and services. The current shift toward an emphasis on software, database management, and end-user tools in the computer and telecommunication industries tend to highlight the increasing importance of content and knowledge rather than just information dissemination. Customization of information services, creating packaging and repackaging of information, and information brokering services that add value to the product emphasize that information is an economic resource.

KNOWLEDGE MANAGEMENT

Information professionals have primarily focused on acquiring, organizing, storing, and preserving prepackaged information. More emphasis was placed on bibliographic control and the dissemination of information than on the creation, diffusion, and utilization of information. They were less concerned with content and knowledge structures. Diagnosing of information needs was done at a distance from the environment in which information was needed for either synthesizing, learning, or decision making.

Knowledge management shifts the information professionals concern from being primarily focused on the storage and retrieval functions to actively participating in the information transfer process. Information transfer is defined as the creation, dissemination, organization, diffusion, and use of information in all formats. It also means that the computer networks serving information professionals must enhance the information transfer processes. Networks and information service providers need to shift from thinking primarily about access to the potential that information has the impact of information. Information transfer is an interactive and dynamic process, as described in Figure 8.1.

Creation. Stephen D. Nelson (1981: 41–78) states that scientific knowledge creation has several dimensions. Knowledge is created in a cultural context influenced by politics, economics, and technology. Knowledge creation is dependent on resources both financial and human. Scientists belong to a discipline, have membership in a professional association,

Figure 8.1
Information Transfer

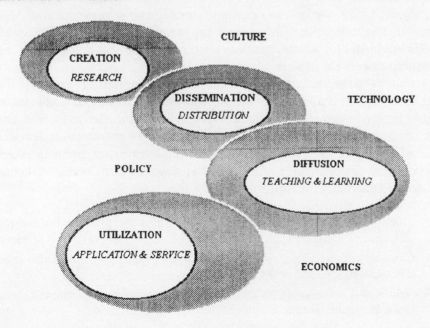

Published with permission of Herbert Achleitner and Brian C. O'Connor.

ascribe to a particular value system, and adhere to official information channels.

Dissemination. Susan S. Klein and Margaret K. Gwaltney (1991: 241–265) trace the development of the dissemination system. This begins with a one-way spreading of information and helps the user seek and acquire alternative sources of information and learn about options. The next level is interactive and provides for a multidirectional flow of information into a system that leads to implementation and use of knowledge.

Diffusion. Diffusion models are useful in helping to understand the complexity of people's information seeking, sharing, and gathering behavior. Diffusion theory is particularly useful in understanding information needs and helps in the design of information delivery systems. This helps determine how current, accessible, understandable, and practical the information should be. This is particularly important in a culturally and socioeconomically diverse society such as ours (Chatman 1986: 377–386).

Utilization. Knowledge utilization aims at increasing the employment of knowledge to solve problems and improve the quality of life. According to Thomas E. Backer (1991: 225–240), it is a broad field encompassing areas such as technology transfer, dissemination and diffusion, research utilization, sociology of knowledge, organizational change, and policy research. Utilization involves designing strategies that help put knowledge to use. Institutions, such as research universities and research and development institutes, where creativity and innovation is a high priority can benefit from these models.

Critical to the understanding of the information transfer process is the realization that it allows the information professional to be dominant in the shaping of knowledge structures. Applying social science theories and models in the design, testing, and evaluation of information services results in a proactive system. The American Information Industry Association developed a guide of information services (Zurkowski 1984) that includes the following information packages:

- *Content services*. News services, databases, libraries, information brokers, electronic database providers, financial services, and electronic mail services.
- *Content packages*. Books, journals, newsletters, magazines, film, videotapes, disks, CD-ROMs, and WORMS.
- *Information technologies*. Computers, data processing, microforms, laser disks, and optical media.
- *Integrated technologies*. Modems, packet switching, digital switches, gateways, voice systems, and facsimiles.

- *Communication channels.* Post office, telephone, cable, satellite, cellular services, paging services, and international record carriers.
- *Broadcast channels.* TV networks, radio, teletext, and multiple distribution services.

Information services in the future merge content packages, information technology, communications, and integrating technologies (Ardis 1994: vi). But more importantly, this merging of technologies will be accomplished in the service of enhancing the information transfer process. This has been conceptualized by Roger B. Wyatt (1994) in the matrix shown in Figure 8.2.

This matrix incorporates the information transfer process and the merging of the various information technologies. Richard E. Lucier (1990: 24–31) discusses how this works at the University of California, San Francisco library. He emphasizes that dissemination is facilitated by high-speed data communications networks driven by user needs in a global environment. Knowledge is customized to specific disciplines. Currency, accuracy, and integrity are valued. A variety of software is available and, to facilitate the use of software, training sessions are part of the service component of the library. Multimedia software to support the diffusion of knowledge is also an important component of such a system. Finally, the system has to be interactive to allow for collaboration and encourage knowledge production.

Figure 8.2
The Information Transfer Process

	COMPUTERS	MASS STORAGE	VIDEO	AUDIO
CREATION				
DISSEMINATION				
DIFFUSION				
ORGANIZATION				
UTILIZATION				

THOUGHTWARE   *HARDWARE*   *SOFTWARE*

Published with permission of Herbert Achleitner and Brian C. O'Connor.

EDUCATIONAL TRENDS

The evolution of information centers and systems for storing and retrieving information to management knowledge centers requires a different information professional with a different knowledge base. Donald A. Marchand and Forest W. Horton, Jr. (1986: 236) identify six categories of information professionals. The following list is an adaptation.

- *Information theorists*. Concerned with the content, values, and methodologies of paradigms, they focus on the sociology of information, psychology of information use, information engineering, and the management of information organizations.

- *Information brokers*. While diagnosing clients' information needs and customizing the delivery of information packets, brokers focus on value-in-use; that is, information has value only if it is appropriate to the task (Cronin and Davenport 1991: 69).

- *Information engineers*. In order to analyze client's needs, information processing and usage patterns, information problems, and design, implement, and evaluate the effectiveness of employed systems, information engineers maintain data/knowledge bases and install, operate, and control hardware and software.

- *Information intermediaries*. While providing linkage between the user and the source of knowledge, they help the user become knowledgeable.

- I*nformation managers*. As decision makers, they provide the leadership necessary to align constituencies around common understandings of the new goals of information technology, the new global order, and the new enterprise, which function in an open, networked, dynamic information environment.

- *Educators of information professionals*. In education and research, they create new knowledge and provide relevant education, consulting, and training to professionals listed here as well as to non-professional information workers.

The preceding takes a very broad view of who and what make up information professionals. It recognizes that information professionals are in the knowledge transfer business and deeply affected by changing information technology. The information economy will require all the knowledge areas, tools, and skills listed. This may imply continuous education in electronic information work and learning to navigate in and benefit from the digital environment.

CONCLUSION

We cannot escape the dynamics surrounding us. The changing technology, and the globalization of information impact the very foundations of information organizations and professionals. In focusing on changing values, information technology, and telecommunications, this impact suggests such questions as

- How is the profession changing?
- How are information organizations affected by changing technology?
- How are information organizations responding and what innovative models exist?
- How is the way we work and interact changing?
- How do we coordinate across multiple cultures and languages?
- Who will help—who are the partners that enable this transformation?

Some broad conclusions can be drawn. In order to provide up-to-date educational experiences, library and information management schools must forge linkages with emerging information streams. Partnerships with, for example, the Information Brokers Association and the Information Industry Association can serve as a means of monitoring industry trends and educational needs. Associations that are highly entrepreneurial and technology dependent are good sources for future trend analysis.

Similar partnerships with both developed and developing nations can equally serve as sources of process. Going beyond educating foreign students and working toward exchanges of educators and professionals builds networks and allows for the analysis of information transfer from other perspectives. The emergent paradigm values multiple perspectives as a way of solving complex problems. Primary experience in another culture and learning another language will be valued enormously in a networked world where anywhere and anyplace communication is quickly becoming the norm.

The values that we have inherited stem from the print world and have linked us closely to the humanities and social sciences. Today, the business and technology paradigm are the driving forces of change and transformation. The insatiable demand for more information and the concomitant ability to deliver large quantities are creating unique situations of almost simultaneous conditions of information overload and action as a result of the energy released by information. A good example can be seen with the recent conflict in the Middle East, where the U.S. military processed huge quantities of data, visual information, and intelligence successfully. The trend is clear: rather than storing and retrieving information, the next step is toward ferreting out, compressing, manipulating, juxtaposing, repackaging, and synthesizing information. It is to this end that we need to educate future professionals.

NOTE

The author wishes to acknowledge the assistance of Brian C. O'Connor in the development of Figures 8.2 and 8.3.

REFERENCES

Achleitner, Herbert K. and Martha L. Hale. 1988. "Information Transfer: Educating Information Professionals in the Emerging Paradigm." In Savad, Rejean (ed.) Proceedings of the First Joint Meeting Between the Associations International des Ecoles de Sciences de l'informative and the Association for Library and Information Science Education. Montreal, Canada.

Ardis, Susan B. (comp.) 1994. *Library Without Walls: Plug in and Go*. Washington, D.C.: Special Library Association.

Backer, Thomas E. 1991. "Knowledge Utilization: The Third Wave." *Knowledge: Creation, Diffusion, Utilization* 12(3): 225–240.

Bradley, Stephen P., Jerry A. Hausman, and Richard L. Nolan. 1993. *Globalization, Technology, and Competition: The Fusion of Computers and Telecommunications in the 1990s*. Boston: Harvard Business School Press.

Chatman, Elfreda A. 1986. "Diffusion Theory: A Review and Test of a Conceptual Model in Information Diffusion." *Journal of the American Society for Information Science*, 37(6): 377–386.

Cronin, Blaise and Elisabeth Davenport. 1991. *Elements of Information Management*. Metuchen, NJ: The Scarecrow Press, Inc.

Davis, Stanley M. 1987. *Future Perfect*. Reading, MA: Addison-Wesley.

Drucker, Peter F. 1989. *The New Realities*. New York: Harper & Row.

Drucker, Peter F. 1993. Post-Capitalist Society. New York: Harper Business.

Harasim, Linda M. (Ed.). 1994. *Global Networks: Computers and International Communication*. Cambridge, MA: The MIT Press.

Klein, Susan S. and Margaret K. Gwaltney. 1991. "Charting the Education Dissemination System: Where We Are and Where We Go From Here." *Knowledge: Creation, Diffusion, Utilization* 12(3): 241–265.

Kuhn, Thomas S. 1970. *The Structure of Scientific Revolutions*. Chicago: The University of Chicago Press.

Lucier, Richard E. 1990. "Knowledge Management: Refining Roles in Scientific Communication." *EDUCOM Review* 25(3): 21–27.

Nelson, Stephen D. 1981. "Knowledge Creation: An Overview." In Robert F. Rich (Ed.). *The Knowledge Cycle*. Beverly Hills, CA: Sage.

Marchand, Donald A. and Forest W. Horton, Jr. 1986. *Infotrends: Profiting from Your Information Resources*. New York: John Wiley & Sons.

Ray, Michael and Alan Rinzler. 1993. *The New Paradigm in Business: Emerging Strategies for Leadership and Organizational Change*. New York: Jeremy P. Tarcher/Perigee Books.

Schwartz, Peter and James Ogilvy. 1979. *The Emergent Paradigm: Changing Patterns of Thought and Belief*. Menlo Park. CA: SRI International.

Tapscott, Don and Art Caston. 1993. *Paradigm Shift: The New Promise of Information Technology*. New York: McGraw-Hill Inc.

Wyatt, Roger B. 1994. *The Technology Quartet*. Unpublished manuscript.

Zurkowski, P. G. 1984. "Integrating America's Infrastructure. *Journal of the American Society for Information Science* 35(3): 170–178.

9 Impact on the International Development of Librarianship

Charles Wm. Conaway

The title of this chapter presents some ambiguities. In one sense, "librarianship" is the name of a profession. Interpreted broadly, "librarianship" can be regarded as the constellation of activities that go on inside libraries as they strive to meet the information needs of the constituencies that support them. Without a commitment to this goal, the profession will have little reason to continue to exist except to manage what will increasingly come to look like museums honoring the book.

A further ambiguity is the word "international." On one hand, this could be thought of as a worldwide network of channels in which information flows without regard to the borders of individual countries. On the other hand, the focus could be on the comparative aspects of librarianship as it is practiced in a variety of countries, in which technological innovation moves from country to country at varying speeds and with varying degrees of success as each nation attempts to meet its people's information needs more cost-effectively. This chapter will deal with each of these interpretations in turn.

Although recent political and socioeconomic events, particularly the break-up of the Soviet Union, have brought about dramatic changes in relationships among nations, an older tripartite model still has analytical value. The three clusters are (1) the Western industrialized countries (plus Japan), (2) the former Warsaw Pact countries of eastern Europe, and (3) the so-called Third World developing countries of Latin America and the Caribbean, Africa, and Asia. Although anomalies such as the oil-rich countries of the Middle East and the rapidly industrializing countries of Asia are acknowledged, this model remains adequate for the current discussion.

FACTORS ENCOURAGING OR RETARDING THE DIFFUSION OF TECHNOLOGICAL INNOVATION IN LIBRARIES

In Chapter 2, Johannah Sherrer discussed the pandemic problems of the conservative nature of librarianship regarding change. Of course, this tendency is not unique to members of the library fraternity as individuals. Further, there are a number of other factors that come into play as technological innovation reaches national borders. Among them are the following.

1. *Current state of library development.* At the moment there is great variation in the degree of library development in countries around the world. The reasons for this variation are numerous and deeply rooted. Among them are the absolute lack of resources to support the development of information systems, particularly the parts, such as libraries, that are sometimes regarded as "frills," not essential to national development or to citizens' quality of life. In countries where there are more immediate demands for resources than governmental funders can support, provision of libraries may be regarded as desirable, but unaffordable. These unpleasant economic realities are likely to endure for the foreseeable future in many parts of the world.

2. *Antipathy toward freedom of inquiry.* The cherished view in some democratic countries that any idea may be freely held and discussed is not universally accepted by governments in power. Whether a totalitarian regime is a self-protective dictatorship or a theocracy, easy access to alternative ideas may not be encouraged. Information is understood to be dangerous, and efforts to hinder access to it are more likely to be found than in those regimes that support access to a wide variety of ideas, via telecommunication systems, a vigorous free press, and libraries.

3. *Resistance to "outside" social influences.* The reasons for this are complex. The motivation may be nationalistic in nature, with the goal of protecting and nurturing an indigenous culture or avoiding the perceived "cultural imperialism" of an insidious alien culture. These kinds of issues were widely debated in the failed effort to find an acceptable set of compromises in a New World Information Order during the last decade. Associated with this is not only the philosophical question of whether technology can be culturally neutral, but also whether it inevitably brings with it elements of the culture that creates it.

4. *Protection of national economies.* Information- and technology-exporting countries, like many in the industrialized West, and others attempting to support the development of their national industries, are at cross-purposes. The strenuous efforts of Brazil and India, for example, to develop their own computer industries caused them to discourage strongly the import of useful technology from other countries. Although they are large countries in their own right, there is reason to suspect that they are also motivated by the possibility of becoming the dominant powers in their own regions.

Since computers are often seen as being labor-saving (although, in the library community, this result has rarely been demonstrated), in countries where there is chronic underemployment, increased productivity that causes jobs to be lost is not viewed as a positive feature of new technology.

5. *Lack of effective leadership for library development.* In some cases, there may too few technically competent people in a country, or they may be too deeply buried in the governmental hierarchy to be able to influence decision making. To some degree, this problem may be the result of little exposure to the technology in a working system that could be seen as an appropriate model for adoption or adaptation to help meet local needs.

6. *Vernacular interface languages.* The transferability of information technology is often reduced because the user interfaces are written in a language that is not the vernacular of the people who will be using the system. Being forced to use a "foreign language" to find information, even when that which is being sought is in one's own language, is not only a cultural affront, it often presents a very practical problem as well. For example, in countries where English is a common second language, it is often so only for the well-educated fraction of the population and, even then, many information seekers prefer to use their own mother tongue. To translate an English interface into Spanish or French is rarely a serious problem, but to translate one effectively into Korean, Arabic, Serbo-Croatian, or other languages not using the Latin alphabet is a much more difficult challenge. An awkward compromise is often two independent, parallel bibliographic systems.

7. *Current state of international standards.* Although progress is clearly being made in the development of national standards such as the Z39.50 NISO protocol and its extensions, progress on international versions through the ISO process, by necessity, will be slower. Although incompatibility of electrical current has been worked around effectively, these problems will continue to deter easy adoption of information technology in some places where, at times, even a reliable electricity supply is problematic.

8. *Post, telephone, and telegraph (PTT) monopolies*. The PTT monopolies that exist in many countries have both positive and negative effects. On the positive side, the monopoly can increase standardization. There are many negative aspects, however. Among them are discouragement of entrepreneurial activity, a tendency to control the content of the messages, and tariff-setting at relatively high rates. The last is a particularly perverse tendency.

Any monopoly, of course, allows costs to be set at "whatever the traffic will bear." Traditionally, these monopolies have been relatively easy to enforce and have been used by governmental agencies to raise revenue to support the general activities of government, not just for the maintenance and improvement of the information infrastructure. Thus, information that might be very useful to have for national development is hindered by the high costs of remote access.

At the moment, two counter-trends are developing. First, there is a tendency for the PTT monopolies to be extended to the newer technologies such as cable television distribution systems. In the other direction, there is a move, especially noticeable in Mexico, Argentina, Chile, and in several Eastern European countries, to privatize the former state monopolies, in patterns similar to what was seen in the United States during the 1970s and 1980s.

9. *The problem of rising expectations for information*. Although it was rarely written about, even a casual observer of the diffusion of the online searching capability and the growth of the bibliographic utilities in the United States during the late 1960s, 1970s, and early 1980s would have noticed a reluctance to provide information seekers with knowledge of the existence of potentially useful materials. This stemmed from fear that the demand for interlibrary loans would overwhelm the existing library's ability to acquire the desired items. This tendency was often hidden by plausible claims that the telecommunication and connect charges were too expensive to be borne by a library. An unstated—and unflattering—reason was almost certainly, "If we let them find out that the information they seek exists, they will almost certainly request it, and then what will we do?"

With a more sophisticated and demanding clientele and more cost-effective document delivery systems (outlined by George Machovec in Chapter 1), this is less a problem than it was in the past. However, it is reasonable to expect that this is likely to be a major hindrance in those libraries that have very limited resources locally and that will have to rely upon either slow, but relatively economical postal delivery systems to remote locations, or relatively high-cost non-postal systems that provide quicker responses. To some degree, the *deus ex machina* solutions of Internet or fax delivery may ameliorate this problem.

BIBLIOGRAPHIC INSTRUCTION AND REFERENCE SERVICE IN OTHER COUNTRIES

Generally, the challenges that are seen in the United States regarding the attitudes and skills of reference staff members and the need to train information seekers to use new information systems are likely to be echoed in libraries elsewhere. These problems have been discussed previously, especially by Johannah Sherrer (Chapter 2), Harvey Sager (Chapter 3), and John Tyson (Chapter 4) and will not be addressed further here.

THE LIBRARY EDUCATION IMPLICATIONS OF THE DEVELOPMENT OF INTERNATIONAL LIBRARIANSHIP

Thomas Walker and Herbert Achleitner (in Chapters 7 and 8) have dealt with the curricular changes and the necessary attitudinal changes that will be required to train librarians in library schools in the United States. There will also be a considerable amount of reeducation required of professionals currently employed in the field and continuing education for the foreseeable future as even new graduates "age" in their workplaces.

Where the information infrastructure in a country is underdeveloped, so are libraries. Likewise, where libraries are underdeveloped, so is library education. Thus, many of the changes in library school curricula and the needs for continuing education of working librarians will be felt internationally—some simultaneously with the implementation of the new technology, but others in anticipation of advances, and still others on an on-going basis.

Although a lively debate can usually be generated by asking the question "Should library schools lead the development of the profession, or reflect the current realities of the field?" it is very clear that, in the area of library technology, the schools have been driven by developments in the field, and many of them have been rather slow to respond. It is likely that a similar situation will occur in other countries, but there are some actions that can be taken that can smooth the transition from traditional librarianship to a more technologically impacted field.

ACTIVITIES OF ORGANIZATIONS TO FURTHER THE DEVELOPMENT OF LIBRARIANSHIP INTERNATIONALLY

UNESCO—United Nations Education, Scientific, and Cultural Organization

The General Information Programme, known by its French initials as PGI, was crated in 1976 from the merger of a set of existing programs. Its overall goal is to promote the dissemination of information to aid social and economic development, particularly in Third World countries. Its UNISIST program attempts to coordinate development and use of standards, rules, methods, and training approaches internationally.

Promotion of the development of regional information strategies is a principal goal, and it supports this with a variety of activities. Among them are the sponsoring of mainframe and microcomputer software (Comprehensive Display System (CDS) and Integrated Software Invocation System (ISIS)), for bibliographic and other information activities. Spanish, French, and English versions of the software are provided with training in its use. In consultation with the International Federation of Library Associations and Institutions and other international organizations, it designs and coordinates the training information specialists worldwide (Lohner 1993: 828–831).

An overall review of the goals, history, and achievements of UNESCO's activities is presented in *Harmonization of Training in Librarianship, Information Science, and Archives* (1987). It has also developed a modular curriculum for information studies (Large 1987).

IFLA—International Federation of Library Associations and Institutions

In addition to the general promotion of libraries and related institutions and the coordination of international activities, the IFLA has also developed a model curriculum for library schools dealing with technology and its management (Cook, 1987).

ALA—American Library Association

The Office of International Programs is the locus of a variety of activities dealing with the international aspects of librarianship. One of these activities is the Library Fellows Program administered for the U.S.

Information Agency by the ALA. Each year since 1986, a group of librarians has been selected in a very competitive environment to spend a few months to a year working on specific tasks abroad. In a recent "class," fellows were working in Bolivia, Russia, Israel, Iceland, and India among other countries.

The International Relations Roundtable assists foreign visitors to the country, particularly those attending the annual conferences, nominating candidates to serve as delegates to international conferences, and assisting in evaluating credentials for reciprocal placements for foreign librarians to be employed by U.S. libraries and vice versa.

ALISE—Association for Library and Information Science Education

The Library School "Twin" Program is an effort to support library schools in developing countries in whatever ways possible. Although faculty and student exchanges are envisioned, the most typical activity is sending duplicate sets of professional journals for use in the foreign schools' libraries. There is also a Special Interest Group (SIG) on International Library Education.

USIA/USIS—U.S. Information Agency

In addition to a wide variety of propaganda activities, the USIA maintains libraries abroad, usually through local binational foundations, which can serve as models of good practice and successful application of technology. The Benjamin Franklin Library in Mexico City and the Mark Twain Library in San José, Costa Rica, are examples. The USIA also funds the very valuable Library Book Fellows Program described above in the ALA listing. A few experienced librarians and library educators holding terminal degrees are typically awarded Fulbright lectureships each year. There are some similarities between the kinds of assignments they receive and those of the Library Book Fellows.

USAID—U.S. Agency for International Development

Traditional areas of support have been in fields of agriculture and education, including their associated information systems. More recently, the USAID activities have moved toward strengthening democratic institutions and private enterprise development. For example, it contracted with the School of Library and Information Studies at Florida State

University to provide technical expertise under a program designed to strengthen democratic institutions in Peru. The assistance given to a non-public institution was to expand the library building and retrofit existing quarters to take advantage of the newer information technologies. Plans were reviewed in Florida, and two faculty members spent several days on-site in Lima to consult with the library staff and university administrators. Historically, Latin America, Asia, and Africa have been the areas of USAID's greatest involvement. With the break-up of the Warsaw Pact, there has been a shift toward Central and Eastern Europe, and more attention has been given to environmental protection and pollution remediation projects.

USAID has developed microcomputer-based software (MicroSys) which is available to contractors and recipient institutions to facilitate exchange of information between and among organizations in different countries.

AAAS—American Academy for the Advancement of Science

In conjunction with the African Academy of Sciences, AAAS arranges conferences such as the one on electronic networking in Africa recently held in Nairobi (*Electronic Networking in Africa* 1992).

The AAAS also manages the Sub-Saharan Africa Program, which was initially designed to make available scientific journals in conventional formats. However, the current focus is on using computers and CD-ROMs for similar purposes (Levey 1993). Where systems are hardly existing and resources are extremely limited, it is not unusual to see a leap-frogging from a much older state of development to the most current, without passing through the typical intermediate stages.

Partners for the Americas

Partners for the Americas is a continuation of the Partners for Progress programs of the Kennedy administration. It pairs a state or region in the United States with a southern country or region of a larger country for the purpose of mutually beneficial exchanges. For example, Bogotá and northern Colombia are paired with the state of Florida. A member of the Florida State University School of Library and Information Studies served as a consultant to a Colombia-based regional organization to assist in the development of a network of information centers supporting vocational rehabilitation efforts in Latin America. Colombian librarians also are supported by counterparts in Florida when they come north for study tours.

Peace Corps

Professional librarians serving as Peace Corps volunteers find varied assignments. Among recent projects, they have served in Botswana as librarians in secondary schools; in St. Vincent as the Health Librarian in the School of Nursing; and in Malawi, a volunteer created a reference library at the Institute of Management (*Peace Corps Assignment: Library Science* 1992).

Florida International Volunteer Corps

A state-financed parallel to the Peace Corps, this program of the Florida Association for Voluntary Agencies for Caribbean Action (FAVA/CA) matches the skills of volunteers who are residents of Florida with requests for technical assistance from Caribbean countries. A member of the faculty of the Florida State University School of Library and Information Studies recently completed assignments in Belize, Barbados, and St. Lucia under the auspices of FAVA/CA.

Conference of Librarians in International Development

This conference, held every other year at a location in the United States, permits librarians who have had international experience to come together with potential funders, other librarians recently returned from assignments abroad, and other people who are seeking opportunities to work overseas in library development. The first of the conferences was sponsored by Washington State University and the University of Idaho in 1987 in Pullman, Washington. Subsequent meetings were at Indiana University (1989), Oregon State University (1991), and Florida State University (1993). The 1995 conference is scheduled for Kansas City in May and will be sponsored by Emporia State University.

Other Organizations

Other organizations also support library development activities abroad. Among these are the Carnegie Corporation, the Ford Foundation (which recently supported work in South Africa), the Canadian International Development Agency (which frequently works in the Caribbean), the

United Kingdom (which is especially involved in the countries of the Commonwealth), and many other traditional "donor" countries that provide assistance in developing countries. The library school at Aberystwyth in Wales has a long history of preparing librarians from Commonwealth countries.

In the past, the Patrice Lumumba University in Moscow has provided training for nationals of countries in which the former Soviet Union had strategic interests, such as the Gulf States. The German Foundation for International Development has developed a syllabus for librarianship and documentation studies (Hüttemann 1986). The International Monetary Fund and the World Bank also contract for individuals to provide technical assistance in many countries. This includes, for example, Paraguay.

In addition, individual countries also contract with organizations for assistance. For example, after the liberation of Kuwait, the university contracted with the British Library Council to outfit the library buildings and restock the collections. Kuwait University also contracted with a team of three U.S. librarians for additional consulting in the aftermath of the Iraqi invasion, which had resulted in almost complete theft or destruction of more than a dozen libraries and their contents.

PROBLEMS AND STRATEGIES FOR UNITED STATES LIBRARY SCHOOLS IN PREPARING PEOPLE TO RETURN TO THEIR OWN COUNTRIES

These matters were the topic of a session of the 1994 ALISE Conference in Los Angeles. The International Library Education Special Interest Group panel's proceedings unfortunately have not been published. Presenters were Charles Wm. Conaway (Florida State University), Evelyn L. Curry (Texas Woman's University), Consuelo Figueras (University of Puerto Rico), and R. Bernard Welmaker (Clark Atlanta University). Members of the audience also asked useful questions. The following contains some of the ideas that were discussed among the participants:

1. *Identification, recruitment, and support of students from abroad.* What are the characteristics of the students who should be recruited and/or admitted for study in the United States? What sort of preparation should they already have? What expectations do they have? What is the "fit" between their perceived needs and the resources to meet them of the school to which they are applying?

There is evidence that the perceptions of U.S. schools by applicants and their advisors abroad are often vague and that sub-optimal placements are made fairly frequently. Sometimes, a student who wishes to prepare for health science librarianship arrives to study at a university without a medical school or medical library. At other times, an advanced student with a strong commitment to library development in his or her own country arrives at a school in which no faculty member has any except the vaguest knowledge of the student's home country. An advanced student from abroad may have a well-defined research agenda, on the basis of which his or her government supports his or her studies, but arrives here only to discover that library support is virtually non-existent or that no member of the school's faculty has any reading facility in the language of the relevant literature. Clearly, the admissions committee of a school has a responsibility to be mindful of these potential problems, but sometimes the prestige of a high-profile foreign student, an enrollment-driven FTE-productivity formula, a weak application for admission for an undersubscribed program, or a well-intentioned effort to increase diversity in the student body may prove irresistible.

2. *Standard preparation or tailored to individual need?* The simplest thing for a school to do is to treat students in a homogenized way, without regard to their varying backgrounds or needs. Thus, students may come to know the "American way" of librarianship and return home ill-prepared to use this knowledge in a comparatively underdeveloped library system. Of course, one can justify this approach by saying that the student came to study in the United States for just this purpose. But, would he or she not be better served by being given specific guidance on how to implement change in his or her own environment when he or she returns?

3. *Providing practical training during or after classroom instruction before returning home.* Foreign students who have F-1 student visas and have maintained lawful status in the United States for nine consecutive months may apply to the Immigration and Naturalization Service (INS) for a program of "Optional Practical Training" upon the recommendation of their advisors. There are other technical requirements for this program and a student should be advised to seek the advice of a foreign student advisor on campus who keeps current on changes in INS regulations. Changes made on March 19, 1993, are the latest major revisions (Florida State University, International Student Center 1994).

The Mortenson Center for International Library Programs at the University of Illinois at Urbana-Champaign exists specifically for the purpose of supporting foreign librarians while they are studying in the United States. It ordinarily arranges study tours and longer-term placements for more experienced, higher-level administrators.

REFERENCES

Cook, Michael. (1987). *Training in Technology and Its Management.* The Hague: International Federation of Library Associations. [ERIC Document Number: ED299976]

Electronic Networking in Africa: Advancing Science and Technology for Development: Proceedings Volume of a Workshop on Science and Technology Communication Networks in Africa. (1992). Nairobi, Kenya, August 27–29, 186 pp.

Florida State University, International Student Center. (1994). [*Information Packet on J-1 Academic Training*], [Current as of February, 1994].

Harmonization of Training in Librarianship, Information Science and Education. (1987). Paris: UNESCO. General Information Programme March. 13 pp.

Hüttemann, Lutz (ed.) (1986). *Librarianship and Documentation Studies: A Handbook for Teaching and Learning Materials.* Bonn: German Foundation for International Development. [ERIC Document Number: ED279337]

Large, J. A. (1987). *A Modular Curriculum in Information Studies.* Paris: UNESCO. General Information Programme and UNISIST. [ERIC Document Number: ED286512]

Levey, Lisbeth A. (1993). *Computer and CD-ROM Capability in Sub-Saharan African University and Research Libraries.* Washington, DC: American Association for the Advancement of Science. Sub-Saharan Africa Journal Distribution Program. 45 pp.

The Library Fellows Program. (1992?). Chicago: American Library Association. A brochure.

Lohner, Wolfgang. (1993). "Unesco" in *World Encyclopedia of Library and Information Services,* 3rd ed. Chicago: American Library Association, pp. 827–831.

Peace Corps Assignment: Library Science. March 1992. 4 pp.

U.S. Information Ambassadors: The 1991–92 Library Fellows. (1993). Chicago: American Library Association. 26 pp.

Selected Bibliography

Aherns, Judith, and Gerardo A. Esquer. 1993. "Proposal for a Subject Oriented User Interface to the Internet." *Proceedings of INET '93*: DBA 1–10.

American Library Association Presidential Committee on Information Literacy Final Report. 1989. Chicago: American Library Association.

Anderson, Charles. 1990. "Impact of the New Technology on Patrons and Staff." *Wilson Library Bulletin* 64 (February): 69–70.

Arms, C. (Ed.). 1990. *Campus Strategies for Libraries and Electronic Information*. Maynard, MA: Digital Press.

Association of College and Research Libraries/Bibliographic Instruction Section Task Force on Model Statement of Objectives. 1987. "Model Statement of Objectives for Academic Bibliographic Instruction: Draft Revision." *College and Research Libraries News* 48(5): 256–261.

Backer, Thomas E. 1991. "Knowledge Utilization: The Third Wave." *Knowledge: Creation, Diffusion, Utilization* 12(3): 225–240.

Baker, Nicholson. 1994. "Discards." *The New Yorker* (April 4): 64–86.

Baker, Shirley K., and Mary E. Jackson. 1992. *Maximizing Access, Minimizing Cost: A First Step Toward the Information Access Future*. Washington, DC: Association of Research Libraries.

Balas, Janet L. 1993. "OPACs and Much More." *Computers in Libraries* 13(1): 28+.

Barry, Dave. 1994. "The '90s, Looking Back at the Interactive Salad Bar." *Newsweek* (January 3): 53–54.

Becker, J. 1984. "An Information Scientist's View on Evolving Information Technology." *Journal of the American Society for Information Science* 35(3): 64–169.

Behrens, Shirley J. 1992. "Librarians and Information Literacy." *Mousaion* 10: 81–88.

Berners-Lee, T., et al., 1993. "The World-Wide Web Initiative." *Proceedings of INET '93*: DBC 1–5.

Bergquist, William. 1993. *The Postmodern Organization: Mastering the Art of Irreversible Change*. San Francisco: Josey-Bass.

Besterman, Theodore. 1965. *World Bibliography of Bibliographies*. 4th ed. Lausanne: Societas Bibliographica.

Bevilacqua, Ann. 1993. "Research Assistant." In *Bibliographic Instruction in Practice: A Tribute to the Legacy of Evan Ira Farber*. Based on the 5th Earlham College-Eckerd College Bibliographic Instruction Conference, February 5–7, 1992. Ann Arbor: Pierian Press.

Bjorner, Susan N. 1991. "The Information Literacy Curriculum—A Working Model." *IATUL Quarterly* 5 (June): 150–160.

Blair, David C., and M. E. Maron. 1985. "An Evaluation of Retrieval Effectiveness for a Full-Text Document Retrieval System." *Communications of the ACM 28* (March): 289–299.

Blumenschein, Adalbert. ca. 1765–1781. "Beschreibung verschiedener Bibliotheken in Europa." Manuscript, sterreiche Nationalbibliothek (Vienna), Handschriftensammlung MS Ser. nov. 2807–2810.

Bodner, Eric, et al. October 1993. *An Internet Billing Server, MS4 Billing Server Prototype Scope Document*. Pittsburgh, Pennsylvania: Carnegie Mellon University, Information Networking Institute.

Boulanger, M. 1987. "Online Services at the Reference Desk: New Technologies vs. Old Problems." *The Reference Librarian* 15: 269–277.

Bowen, William G. 1992. "Foreward." In Anthony M. Cummings et al., *University Libraries and Scholarly Communication: A Study Prepared for the Andrew W. Mellon Foundation*. Washington, DC: The Association of Research Libraries.

Boykin, J. F. 1991. "Library Automation 1970–1990: From the Few to the Many." *Library Administration and Management* 5: 10–15.

Bradley, Stephen P., Jerry A. Hausman, and Richard L. Nolan. 1994. *Globalization, Technology, and Competition: The Fusion of Computers and Telecommunications in the 1990s*. Boston: Harvard Business School Press.

Bregman, Adeane, and Barbara Mento. 1992. "Reference Roving at Boston College." *College and Research Libraries News* 52 (November): 634–637.

Breivik, Patricia Senn. 1989. "Information Literacy: Revolution in Education." In *Coping with Information Illiteracy: Bibliographic Instruction for the Information Age*. Betsy Baker and Mary Ellen Litzinger, eds. Papers presented at the Seventeenth National LOEX Library Instruction Conference held in Ann Arbor, Michigan, May 4 and 5, 1989. Ann Arbor: Pierian Press.

Breivik, Patricia S., and E. Gordon Gee. 1989. *Information Literacy: Revolution in the Library*. New York: Macmillan Publishing Company.

Bryn, Geffert. 1993. "Community Networks in Libraries: A Case Study of the Freenet P.A.T.H." *Public Libraries* 32: 91+.

Bryne, Alex, and Mary Micco. 1988. "Improving OPAC Subject Access: The ADFA Experiment." *College and Research Libraries* 49 (September): 432–441.

Campbell, Jerry. 1992. "Shaking the Conceptual Foundations of Reference: A Perspective." *Reference Services Review* (Winter): 29–36.

Carnevale, A. P., A. S. Gainer, Meltzer, and S. L. Holland, 1988. "Workplace Basics: The Skills Employees Want." *Training and Development Journal* (October): 20–30.

Carroll, J. B., and J. S. Chall, eds. 1975. *Toward a Literate Society: A Report from the National Academy of Education*. New York: McGraw-Hill.

Champine, George A. 1991. *MIT Project Athena, A Model for Distributed Campus Computing*. Boston, MA: Digital Press.

Chatman, Elfreda A. 1986. "Diffusion Theory: A Review and Test of a Conceptual Model in Information Diffusion." *Journal of the American Society for Information Science* 37(6): 377–386.

CLARITECH Corporation. December 1993. *Notes on CLARITECH*. Pittsburgh, PA: CLARITECH Corporation.

Cook, Michael. 1987. *Training in Technology and Its Management*. The Hague: International Federation of Library Associations. (ERIC Document Number: ED299976)

Cottam, Keith. 1989. "The Impact of the Library Intrapreneur on Technology." *Library Trends* 37: 521–531.

Creth, Sheila. 1994. "Changing Times: The Human & Organization Dimensions." Unpublished.

Cronin, Blaise, and Elisabeth Davenport. 1991. *Elements of Information Management*. Metuchen, NJ: The Scarecrow Press, Inc.

Davis, Stanley M. 1987. *Future Perfect*. Reading, MA: Addison-Wesley.

De Klerk, Ann, and Euster, Joanne R. 1989. "Technology and Organizational Metamorphoses." *Library Trends* 37: 157–168.

Demo, William. 1986. *The Idea of Information Literacy in the Age of High-Tech*. Dryden, NY: Educational Resources Information Center.

Diderot, Denis, and Jean Le Rond d'Alembert. 1757–1780. *Encyclopedie, ou Dictionnaire raissone des sciences, des arts et des metiers*. 35 vols. Paris: David, Briasson, LeBreton, and Durand.

Dillon, Martin, and Patrick Wenzel. 1990. "Retrieval Effectiveness of Enhanced Bibliographic Records." *Library Hi Tech* (no. 3): 43–46.

Drucker, Peter F. 1989. *The New Realities*. New York: Harper & Row.

Drucker, Peter F. 1993. *Post-Capitalist Society*. New York: Harper Business.

Dunn, Kathleen. 1986. "Psychological Needs in Undergraduate Information Seeking Behavior." *College and Research Libraries* (September): 475–481.

Eisenberg, Michael B., and Kathleen L. Spitzer. 1991. *Annual Review of Information Science and Technology* 26: 243–285.

"Electronic Data Sources." 1993. In *World Encyclopedia of Library and Information Services*. Chicago: American Library Association.

Electronic Networking in Africa: Advancing Science and Technology for Development: Proceedings Volume of a Workshop on Science and Technology Communication Networks in Africa. Nairobi, Kenya, August 27–29, 1992.

Emard, J. E. 1976. "An Information Science Chronology in Perspective." *Bulletin of the American Society for Information Science* 2(8): 51–56.

Engle, Mary E., Marilyn Lutz, William W. Jones Jr., Genevieve E. Engel. 1993. *Internet Connections: A Librarian's Guide to Dial-up Access and Use*. Chicago: American Library Association.

Euster, Joanne R. 1992. "The Impact on the Academic Library: Political Issues." In *Information Management and Organization Change in Higher Education: The Impact on Academic Libraries*, Gary M. Pitkin, ed. Westport, CT: Meckler.

Falduto, Ellen F., Kenneth C. Blythe, and Polley Ann McClure. 1994. "The Information Age, the People Factor, and the Enlightener IS Manager." *Cause/Effect* 17 (Spring): 7–9.

Faber, Evan. 1993. "Bibliographic Instruction at Earlham College." In Bibliographic Instruction in Practice: A Tribute to the Legacy of Evan Ira Faber. Based on the 5th Earlham College-Eckerd College Bibliographic Instruction Conference, February 5–7, 1992. Ann Arbor: Pierian Press.

Feinberg, Richard. 1989. "Shorting-Out on Long Term Goals: A Different Perspective on Bibliographic Instruction and Information Literacy." In Coping with Information Illiteracy: Bibliographic Instruction for the Information Age, Betsy Baker and Mary Ellen Litzinger, eds. Paper Presented at the Seventeenth National LOEX Library Instruction Conference held in Ann Arbor, Michigan, May 4 and 5, 1989. Ann Arbor: Pierian Press.

Feinberg, Richard, and Christine King. 1988. "Short Term Library Skills Competencies: Arguing for the Achievable." *College & Research Libraries* 49(1): 24–28.

Florida State University, International Student Center. (1994). (*Information Packet on J-1 Academic Training*). (Current as of February, 1994.)

Ford, Barbara. "Reference Beyond (And Without) the Reference Desk." *College and Research Libraries* 47 (September): 491–494.

Freeman, M. S. 1991. "Pen, Ink, Keys, and Cards: Some Reflections on Library Technology." *College and Research Libraries* 52(4): 329–335.

Gesner, Konrad. 1545. *Bibliotheca universalis*. Zurich.

Getz, Malcom. 1991. "Document Delivery." *The Bottom Line* 5(4): 40–44.

Gilster, Paul. 1993. *The Internet Navigator*. New York: John Wiley & Sons.

Grand Challenges: High Performance Computing and Communication. 1991. Washington, DC: U.S. Research and Development Program.

Hansen, W. J., and C. Haas. 1988. "Reading and Writing with Computers: A Framework for Explaining Differences in Performance." *Communications of the ACM* (September): 1080–1089.

Harasim, Linda M., ed. 1994. *Global Networks: Computers and International Communication*. Cambridge, MA: The MIT Press.

Harman, Donna, ed. 1993. *The First Text REtrieval Conference (TREC-I)*. NIST Special Publication 500-207. Washington, DC: U.S. Government Printing Office.

Harman, Donna, ed. Forthcoming. *The Second Text REtrieval Conference (TREC-II)*. NIST Special Publication. Washington, DC: U.S. Government Printing Office.

Harmonization of Training in Librarianship, Information Science and Education. Paris: UNESCO. General Information Programme, March, 1987,

Harrison, Brian R., and Denise A. Troll. 1993. *Proposal to Rewrite the Library Information System (LIS) Client*. Pittsburgh, PA: Carnegie Mellon University Libraries, Library Automation.

Hellemans, A. 1988. *Timetables of Science*. New York: Simon & Schuster.

Hersh, William R., et a. 1992. "Indexing Effectiveness of Linguistic and Non-Linguistic Approaches to Automated Indexing." *Medinfo* 92, 1402–1408.

Heterick, Robert C. 1993. "Introduction: Reengineering Teaching and Learning." In *Reengineering Teaching and Learning in Higher Education: Sheltered Groves, Camelot, Windmills, and Malls*. Boulder, CO: CAUSE.

Higginbotham, Barbara B. 1990. "You Only Have to Touch the Keys . . . ': Nineteenth Century Visions of Twentieth Technology." *Urban Academic Librarian* 7(2): 40–45.

Hoadley, Irene. 1994. "Somewhere Over the Rainbow: Organizational Patterns in Academic Libraries." In *For the Good of the Order: Essays in Honor of Edward G. Holley*, Delmus E. Williams et al., eds. Westport, CT: JAI Press.

Huttemann, Lutz, ed. 1986. *Librarianship and Documentation Studies: A Handbook for Teaching and Learning Materials*. Bonn: German Foundation for International Development. (ERIC Document Number: ED279337.)

Information Literacy and Education for the 21st Century. 1989. Washington, DC: U.S. National Commission on Libraries and Information Science.

Information 2000: Library and Information Services for the 21st Century, Summary Report of the 1991 White House Conference on Library and Information Services. 1991. Washington, DC: NCLIS.

Jackson, Mary E. 1993. *North American Interlibrary Loan/Document Delivery Project: ILL/DD Management System Description*. Washington, DC: Association of Research Libraries.

Jackson, S. L., E. B. Herling, and E. J. Josey, eds. 1976. *A Century of Library Service: Librarianship in the United States & Canada*. Chicago: American Library Association.

Jackson-Brown, Grace. 1993. "The Academic Librarian's New Role as Information Provider." *Reference Librarian* 39: 77–83.

Kayser, Albrecht Christoph. 1790. *Uber die Manipulation bey der Einrichtung einer Bibliothek und der Verfertigung der Bucherverzeichnisse. . . .* Bayreuth: Verlag der Zeitungsdruckerei.

Kilgour, F. G. 1987. "Historical Note: A Personalized Prehistory of OCLC." *Journal of the Society for Information Science* 38(5): 381–384.

King, David, and Betsy Baker. 1987. "Human Aspects of Library Technology: Implications for Academic Library User Education." *Bibliographic Instruction: The Second Generation*, Constance A. Mellon, ed. Littleton, CO: Libraries Unlimited, Inc.

Kirsch, Irwin S., Ann Jungeblut, Lynn Jenkins and Andrew Kolstad. 1993. *Adult Literacy in America*. Washington, DC: U.S. Department of Education, National Center for Education Statistics.

Klein, Susan S., and Margaret K. Gwaltney. 1991. "Charting the Education Dissemination System: Where We Are and Where We Go From Here." *Knowledge: Creation, Diffusion, Utilization* 12 (3): 241–265.

Krol, Ed. 1992. *The Whole Internet: User's Guide & Catalog*. Sebastopol, CA: O'Reilly & Associates, Inc.

Kuhn, Thomas S. 1970. *The Structure of Scientific Revolutions*. Chicago: The University of Chicago Press.

Lane, Elizabeth, and Craig Summerhill. 1993. *Internet Primer for Information Professionals*. Westport, CT: Meckler.

Large, J. A. 1987. *A Modular Curriculum in Information Studies*. Paris: UNESCO. General Information Programme and UNISIST. (ERIC Document Number: ED286512)

Larsen, Patricia. 1991. "The Climate of Change; Library Organizational Structures, 1985–1990." *Reference Librarian* 37: 79–93.

Leach, Ronald G. 1993. "Electronic Document Delivery: New Options for Libraries." *The Journal of Academic Librarianship* 18(6): 359–364.

Leong, John. 1992. *The Andrew II Project: Functional Requirements.* Pittsburgh, PA: Carnegie Mellon University, Computing Services.

Levey, Lisbeth A. 1993. *Computer and CD-ROM Capability in Sub-Saharan African University and Research Libraries.* Washington, DC: American Association for the Advancement of Science. Sub-Saharan Africa Journal Distribution Program.

The Library Fellows Program. 1992. Chicago: American Library Association. (A brochure.)

Lohner, Wolfgang. 1993. "Unesco" in *World Encyclopedia of Library and Information Services*, 3rd ed., pp. 827–831. Chicago: American Library Association.

Lowry, Anita. 1994. "The Information Arcade, University of Iowa Libraries." In *Managing Information Technology as a Catalyst of Change: Proceedings of the 1993 CAUSE Annual Conference, December 7–10, San Diego, California.* Boulder, CO: CAUSE.

Lowry, Charles B. 1993. "Managing Technology: Perspectives and Prospects for a New Paradigm." *Journal of Academic Librarianship* 19 (September): 237–38, 246.

Lucier, Richard E. 1990. "Knowledge Management: Refining Roles in Scientific Communication." *EDUCOM Review* 25(3): 21–27.

Lynch, Beverly P. 1978. "Libraries as Bureaucracies." *Library Trends* 26: 259–267.

Machovec, George S. 1989. "Locally Loaded Databases in Arizona State University's Online Catalog Using the CARL System." *Information Technology and Libraries* 8(2): 161–171.

Machovec, George S. 1990. "The NPTN and the Cleveland Free-Net Community Computer System." *Online Libraries and Microcomputers* 8(11): 1–4.

Machovec, George S. 1993. *Telecommunications, Networking and Internet Glossary.* Chicago: American Library Association.

MacKinnon, Sylvia Carson, et al. 1993. "Z39.50 and LIAS: Penn State's Experience." *Information Technology and Libraries* 12 (June): 230–237.

Martin, James. 1981. *Computer Networks and Distributed Processing: Software, Techniques, Architecture.* Englewood Cliffs, NJ: Prentice-Hall, Inc.

Martin, Susan K. 1989. "Library Management and Emerging Technology: The Immovable Force and the Irresistible Object." *Library Trends* 37 (Winter): 374–382.

Massey-Burzio, Virginia. 1992. "Reference Encounters of a Different Kind: A Symposium." *Journal of Academic Librarianship* 18(5): 276–286.

McCrank, Lawrence S. 1992. "Academic Programs for Information Literacy: Theory and Structure" *RQ.* 31 (Summer): 485–497.

McKinin, Emma Jean, et al. 1991. "The Medline/Full-Text Research Project." *Journal of the American Society for Information Science* 42 (May): 297–307.

McLean, Neil. 1994. "The Management of Information Access in Higher Education." *Cause/Effect* 17 (Spring): 43–46.

Mooers, C. N. 1976. "Technology of Information Handling—A Pioneer's View." *Bulletin of the American Society for Information Science* 2(8): 18–21.

Moran, Barbara B. 1984. *Academic Libraries: The Changing Knowledge Center of Colleges and Universities.* Washington, DC: Association for the Study of Higher Education.

Moran, Barbara. 1994. "What Lies Ahead for Academic Libraries? Steps on the Way to the Virtual Library." In F*or the Good of the Order: Essays in Honor of Edward G. Holley*, Delmus E. Williams et al., eds. Westport, CT: JAI Press.

Morris, James, et al. 1986. "Andrew: A Distributed Personal Computing Environment." *Communications of the ACM* 29 (March): 184–201.

Murray, Philip C. 1993. "Documentation Goes Digital." *Byte* (September): 121–129.

Naito, Marilyn. 1991. "An Information Literacy Curriculum: A Proposal." *College and Research Libraries News* 52 (May): 293–296.

Natke, Nora Jane. 1992. "Emerging Technologies in Resource Sharing and Document Delivery." *Journal of Youth Services in Libraries* 5 (Winter): 189–192.

Nelson, Stephen D. 1981. "Knowledge Creation: An Overview." In *The Knowledge Cycle*, Robert F. Rich, ed. Beverly Hills, CA: Sage.

Nielsen, Brian, and Betsy Baker. 1987. "Educating the Online Catalog User: A Model Evaluation Study." *Library Trends* (Spring): 571–585.

Normore, L. F. 1982. "Human Factors Considerations in Designing Information Retrieval Systems Interfaces: Some Techniques for Lessening User Effort." *Proceedings of the ASIS Annual Meeting* 19: 217–219.

Oberg, Larry. 1992. "Responses to Hammond: Paraprofessionals at the Reference Desk: The End of the Debate." *The Reference Librarian* 37: 105–107.

O'Conner, Roy. 1994. "Macintosh Revolution Battling New Roadblocks." *Arizona Republic* (January 30): H:2.

Olsen, Jan K., and Bill Coons. 1989. *Information Literacy Issue Paper.* Chicago: American Library Association.

Peace Corps Assignment: Library Science. March 1992.

Pizer, I. H. (1984). "Looking Backward, 1984–1959: Twenty-five Years of Library Automation—A Personal View." *Bulletin of the Medical Library Association* 72(4): 335–348.

Plesser, Ronald L., and E. W. Cividanes. 1993. *Serving Citizens in the Information Age: Access Principles for State and Local Government Information.* Washington, DC: Information Industry Association.

Potter, William Gray. 1989. "Expanding the Online Catalog." *Information Technology and Libraries* 8(2): 99–104.

Pritchard-Schoch, Teresa. 1993. "Natural Language Comes of Age." *Online* (May): 33–43.

Quint, Barbara. 1993. "Easy Does It." *Wilson Library Bulletin* (June): 86–91.

RMG Consultants, Inc. 1992. "OSI, Z39.50, and Library Automation." *Papers on Library Automation* (December).

Rader, Hannelore, and Bill Coons. 1989. *Information Literacy Background, Learning Goals and Objectives.* Chicago: American Library Association.

Ranganathan, S. R. 1965. *The Colon Classification.* New Brunswick, NJ: Rutgers University, Graduate School of Library Service.

Ray, Michael and Alan Rinzler. 1993. *The New Paradigm in Business: Emerging Strategies for Leadership and Organizational Change.* New York: Jeremy P. Tarcher/Perigee Books.

Reece, Ernest J. 1936. *The Curriculum in Library Schools.* New York: Columbia University Press.

Report Brief. 1993. Washington, DC: U.S. Congress. Office of Technology Assessment. (November).

Riggs, Donald E. 1993. "Managing Quality: TQM in Libraries." *Library Administration & Management* 7 (Spring): 73–78.

Roszak, Theodore. 1986. "Partners for Democracy: Public Libraries and Information Technology." *Wilson Library Bulletin* 60 (February): 14–17.

Salton, Gerard. 1989. *Automatic Text Processing: The Transformation, Analysis, and Retrieval of Information by Computer.* Reading, MA: Addison-Wesley.

Schwartz, Peter, and James Ogilvy. 1979. *The Emergent Paradigm: Changing Patterns of Thought and Belief.* Menlo Park, CA: SRI International.

Shera, J. H. 1976. "Two Centuries of American Librarianship." *Bulletin of the American Society for Information Science* 2(8): 39–40.

Shill, Harold B. 1987. "Bibliographic Instruction: Planning for the Electronic Information Environment." *College & Research Libraries* 48(5): 433–453.

Sloan, Bernard G. 1991. *Linked Systems for Resource Sharing.* Boston, MA: G.K. Hall & Co.

Smalley, Joseph. 1991. "The French Cataloging Code of 1791: A Translation." *Library Quarterly* 61: 1–14.

Smith, Elizabeth S. 1993. "On the Shoulders of Giants: From Boole to Shannon to Taube: The Origins and Development of Computerized Information from the Mid-19th Century to the Present." *Information Technology and Libraries* 12 (June): 217–226.

Stovel, Lennie, et al. 1993. "RLG's Z39.50 Server: Development and Implementation Issues." *Information Technology and Libraries* 12 (June): 227–230.

Strategic Plan for the Future of Library Science in Massachusetts. 1993. Boston: Massachusetts Board of Library Commissioners.

Sullivan, Laura A., and Nancy F. Campbell. 1991. "Strengthening the Foundation for Information Literacy in an Academic Library." *Reference Librarian* 33: 183–189.

Tapscott, Don, and Art Coston. 1993. *Paradigm Shift: The New Promise of Information Technology.* New York: McGraw-Hill, Inc.

Tedd, L. A. 1987. "Progress in Documentation—Computer-Based Library Systems: A Review of the Last Twenty-One Years." *Journal of Documentation* 43(2): 145–165.

Tenopir, Carol. 1993. "Natural Language Searching with WIN." *Library Journal* (November 1): 55–56.

Thompson, D. Seymour. 1931. "Do We Want a Library Science?" *Library Journal* 56: 743–746.

Troll, Denise A. September 1993. *Z39.58 Search Syntax, a Report.* Pittsburgh, PA: Carnegie Mellon University, University Libraries.

Troll, Denise A. 1993. *Project Mercury & the Development of the Library Information System.* Mercury Technical Report Series, Number 7. Pittsburgh, PA: Carnegie Mellon University.

Turner, Fay. 1990. "The Interlibrary Loan Protocol: An OSI Solution to ILL Messaging." *Library Hi Tech.* Issue 32: 73–82.

U.S. Information Ambassadors: The 1991–92 Library Fellows. 1993. Chicago: American Library Association.

Van Orden, Richard. 1993. "Content-Enriched Access to Electronic Information: Summaries of Selected Research." *Library Hi Tech* (no. 3): 27–32.

Wagner, Richard. 1850/1914. "Das Kunstwerk der Zukunft." In *Samtliche Schriften und Dichtungen.* 6th ed. Vol. 3. pp. 42–177. Leipzig: Breitkopf & Harter.

Waples, Douglas. 1931. "The Graduate Library School, University of Chicago." *Library Quarterly* 1: 26–36.

Ward-Callaghan, Linda. 1987. "The Effect of Emerging Technologies on Children's Library Service." *Library Trends* 35 (Winter): 437–447.

Waters, Donald J. 1991. *From Microfilm to Digital Imagery, a Report of the Yale University Library to the Commission on Preservation and Access.* Washington, DC: Commission on Preservation and Access, Association of Research Libraries.

Wessling, Julie. 1992. "Document Delivery: A Primary Service for the Nineties." *Advances in Librarianship* 16: 1–31.

White, Carl M. 1961. *The Origins of the American Library School.* Metuchen, NJ: Scarecrow.

White, Carl M. 1976. *A Historical Introduction to Library Education: Problems and Progress to 1951.* Metuchen, NJ: Scarecrow.

White, Herbert. 1993. "Scholarly Publication, Academic Libraries, and the Assumption That These Processes are Really under Management Control." *College and Research Libraries* (July): 293–301.

Williamson, Charles C. 1923. *Training for Library Science.* Boston: Merrymount Press. Also published in *The Williamson Reports* of 1921 and 1923. Metuchen, NJ: Scarecrow, 1971.

Wilson, Lizabeth A. 1992. "Changing Users: Bibliographic Instruction for Whom." In *The Evolving Educational Mission of the Library,* Betsy Baker and Mary Ellen Litzinger, eds. Chicago: Bibliographic Instruction Section, Association of College & Research Libraries, A division of the American Library Association.

Wittig, Constance, and Dietmar Wolfram. 1994. "A Survey of Networking Education in North American Library Schools." *Library Trends* 42 (Spring 1994): 626–637.

Woodsworth, Anne, and Theresa Maylone. 1993. *Reinvesting in the Information Job Family: Context, Changes, New Jobs, and Models for Evaluation and Compensation.* Boulder, CO: CAUSE.

Wyatt, Roger B. 1994. *The Technology Quartet.* Unpublished manuscript.

Zurkowski, P. G. 1984. "Integrating America's Infrastructure." *Journal of the American Society for Information Science* 35(3): 170–178.

Index

About the Contributors

HERBERT K. ACHLEITNER is associate professor in the School of Library and Information Management, Emporia State University in Kansas.

CHARLES Wm. CONAWAY is associate professor in the School of Library and Information Studies, Florida State University in Tallahassee.

CHARLES B. LOWRY is university librarian at Carnegie Mellon University in Pittsburgh, Pennsylvania.

GEORGE MACHOVEC is technical services coordinator for the Colorado Alliance of Research Libraries (CARL) in Denver.

GARY M. PITKIN is dean of university libraries at the University of Northern Colorado in Greeley.

HARVEY SAGER is reference librarian and subject specialist for the Arizona State University Libraries in Tempe.

JOHANNAH SHERRER is director of the Aubrey R. Watzek Library, Lewis and Clark College, in Portland, Oregon.

JOHN C. TYSON is associate professor in the Graduate School of Library and Information Science, University of Tennessee at Knoxville. At the time the chapter was written, he was the Virginia State Librarian.

THOMAS D. WALKER is assistant professor in the School of Library and Information Science, University of Wisconsin at Milwaukee.

DELMUS E. WILLIAMS is dean of university libraries at the University of Akron in Ohio.

ISBN 0-313-29365-1

90000>

EAN

9 780313 293658

HARDCOVER BAR CODE